Animal Mandalas

Coloring Book

Thank you for purchasing our book! We hope you enjoy it and find it useful. If you have a moment, we would love it if you could leave a review so that other readers can hear your thoughts on the book. Thanks again and have a great day!

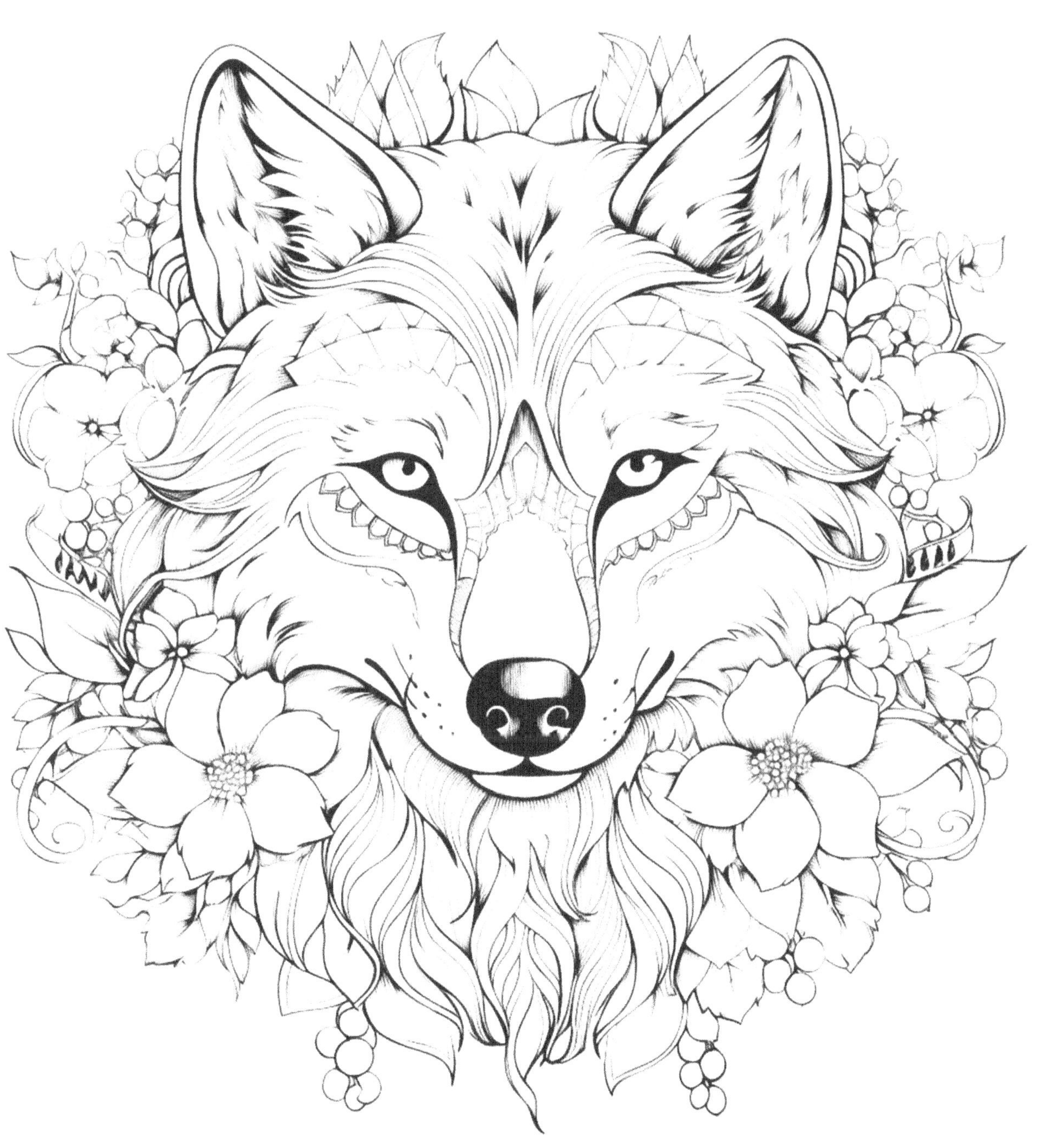

Color Test Pages

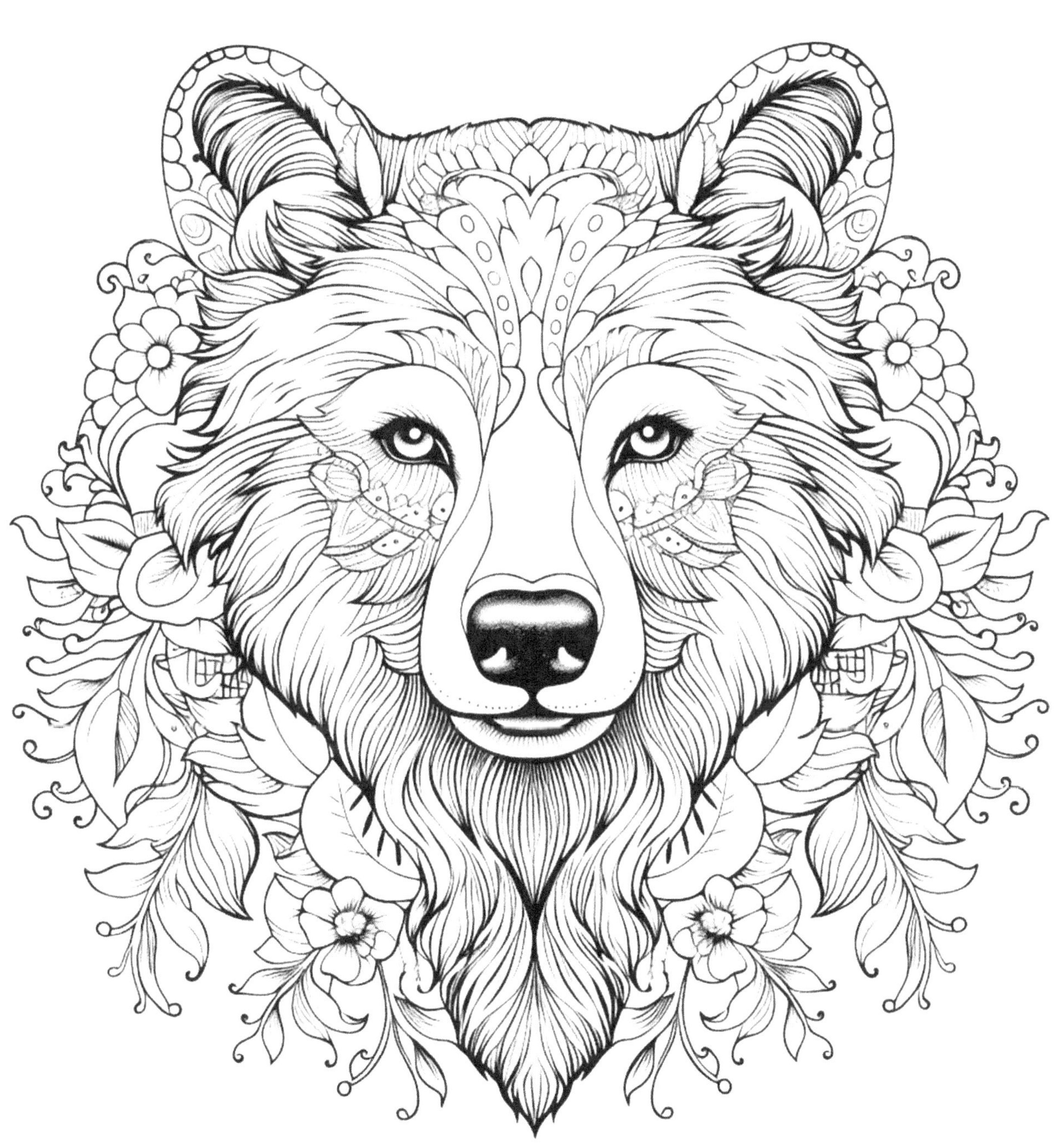

Color Test Pages

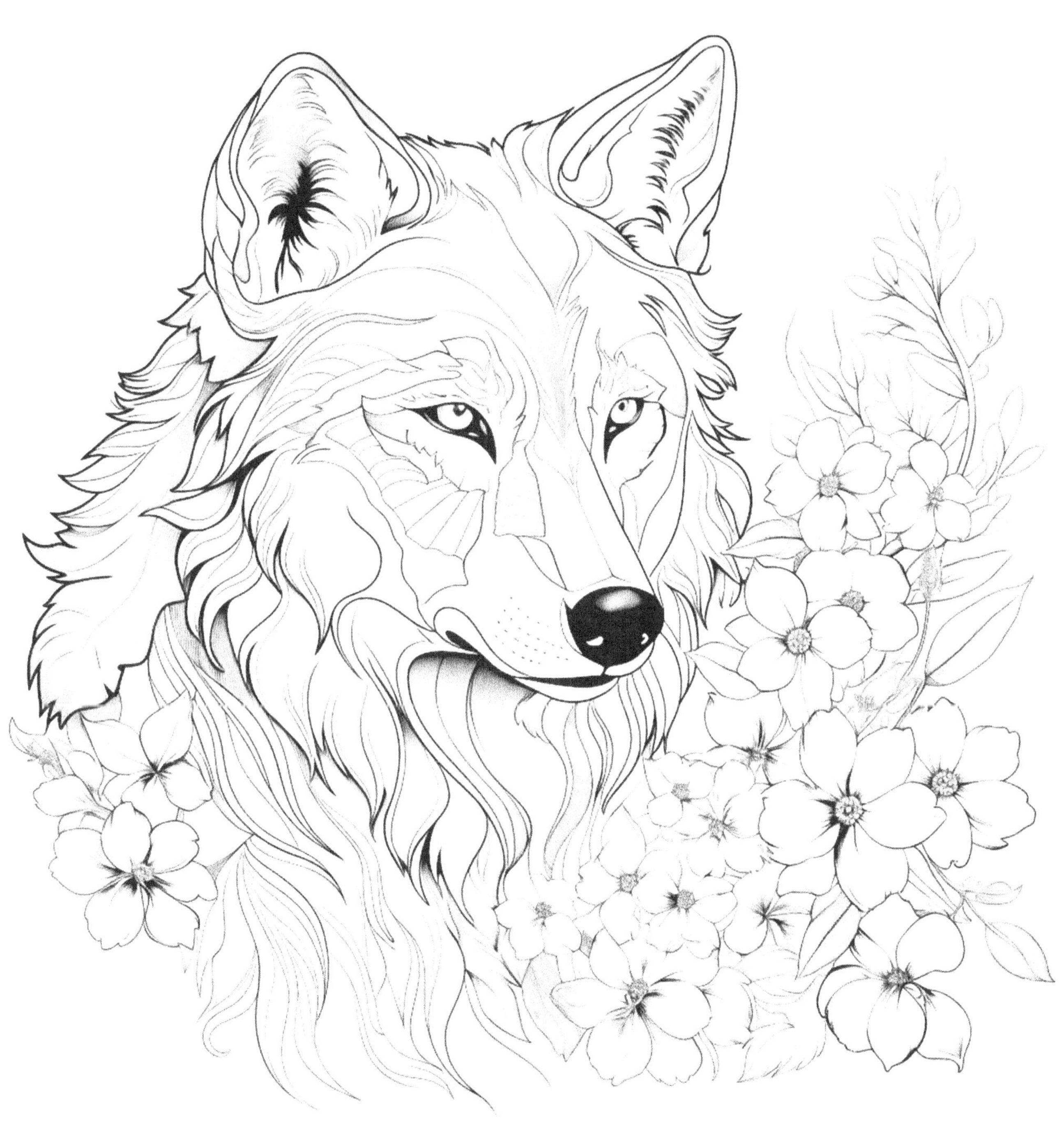

Color Test Pages

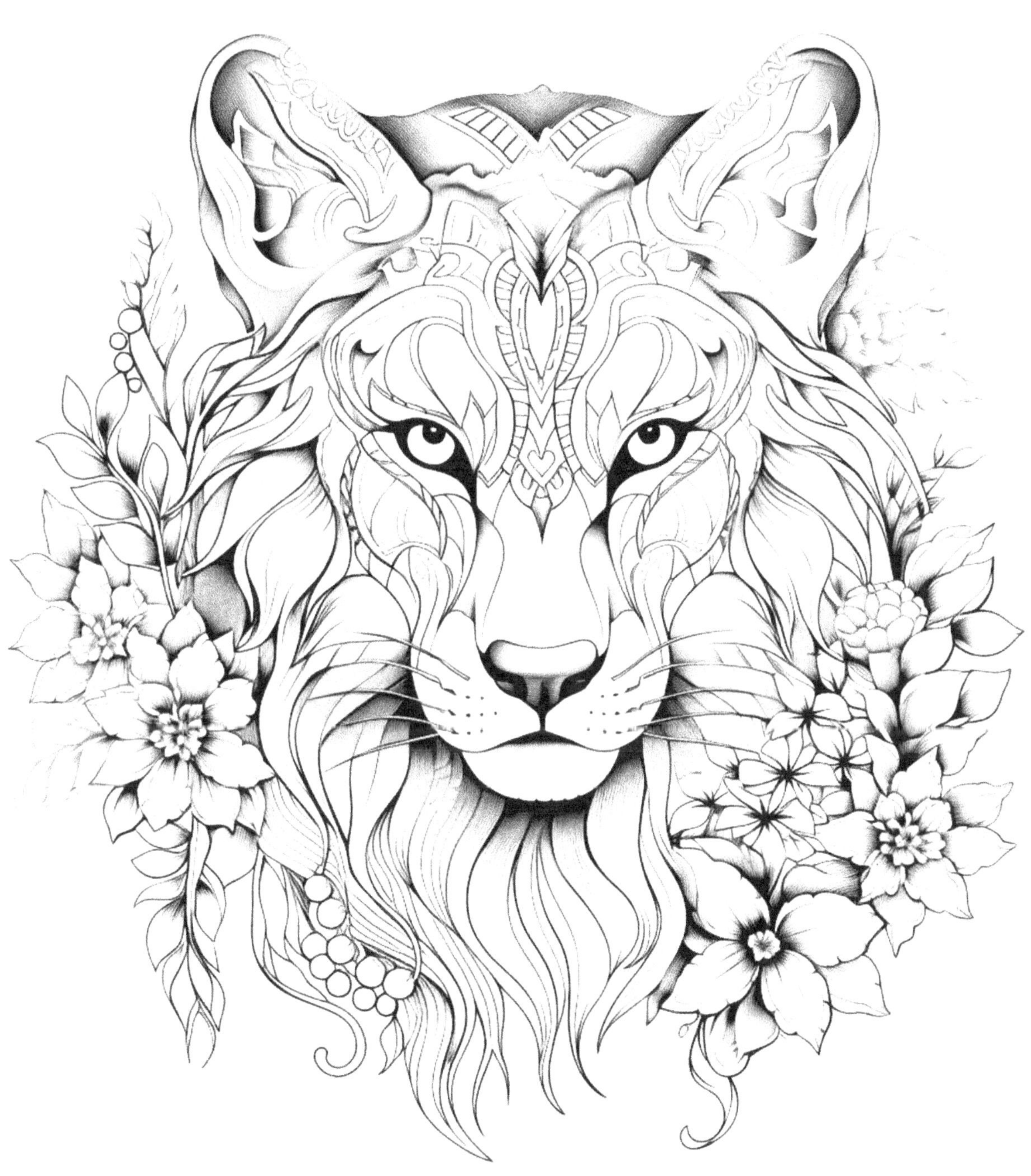

Color Test Pages

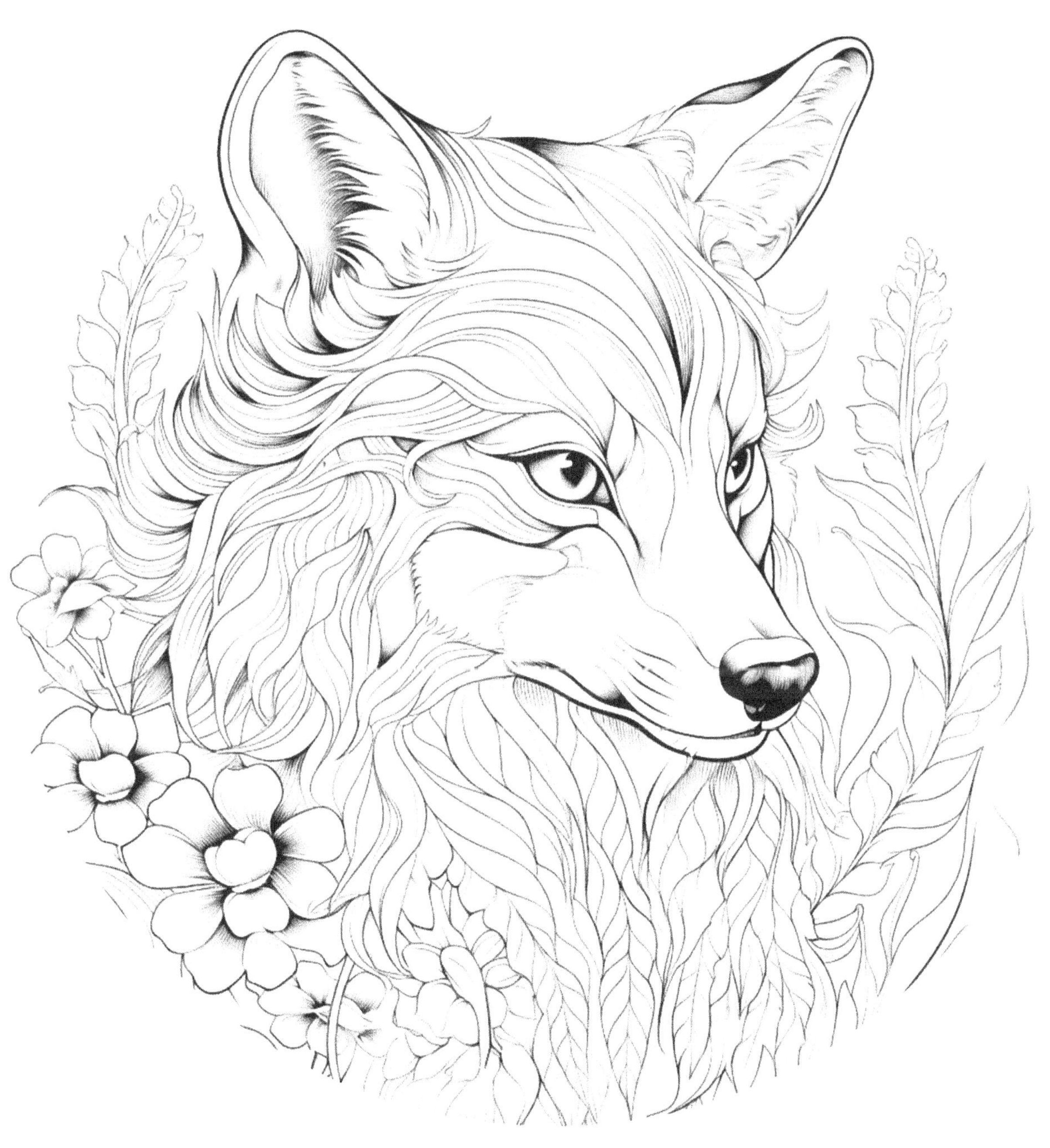

Color Test Pages

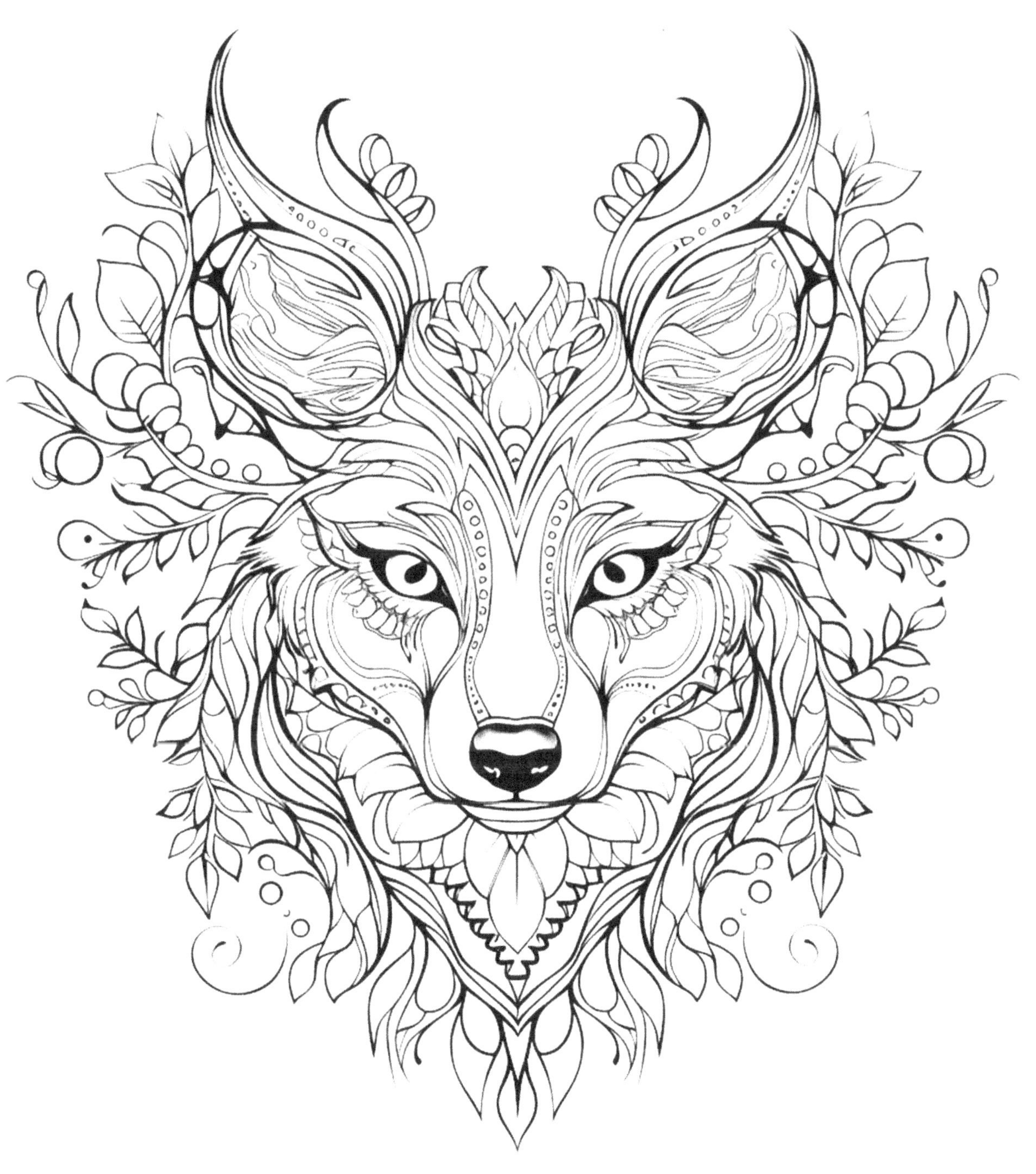

Color Test Pages

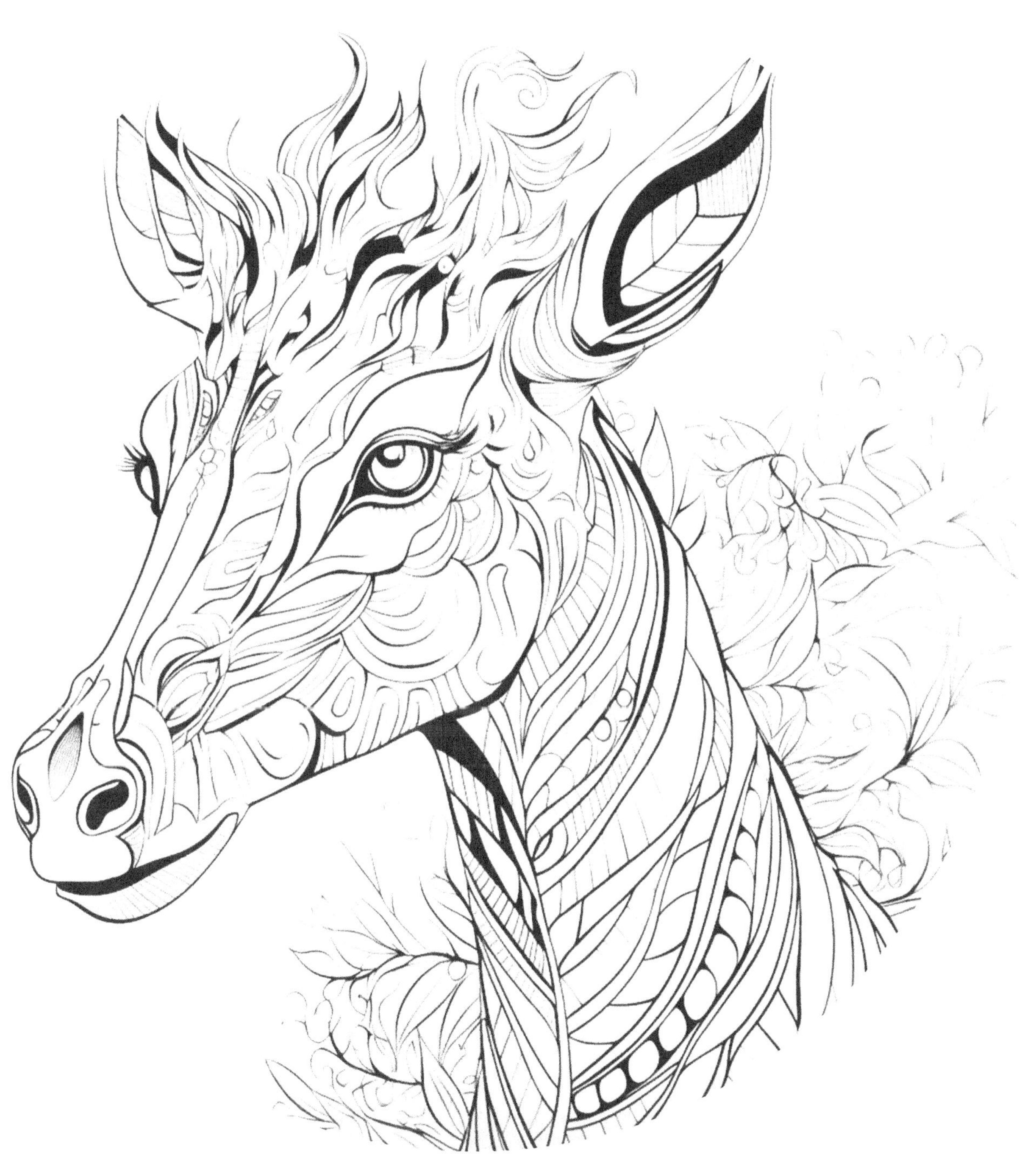

Color Test Pages

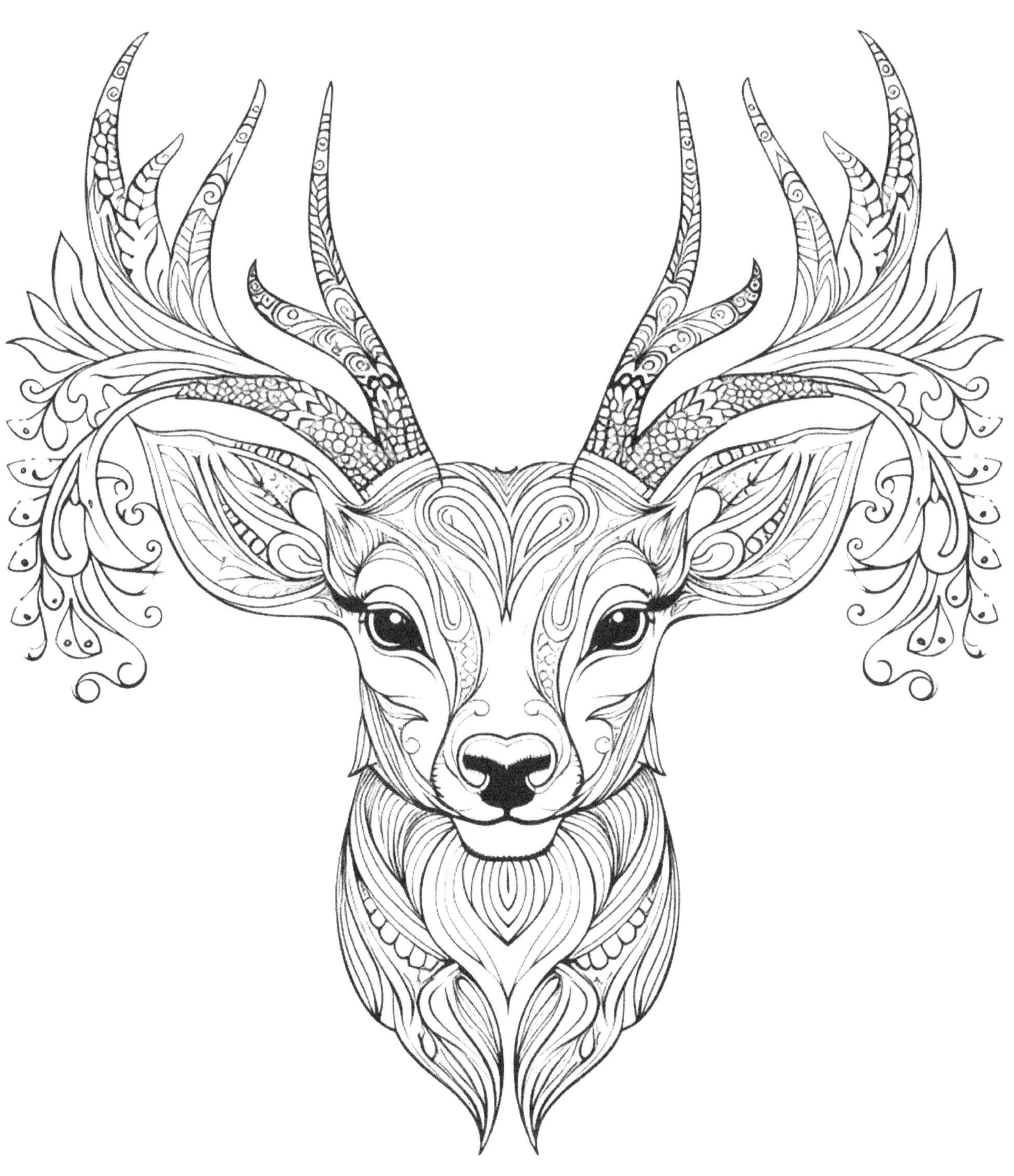

Color Test Pages

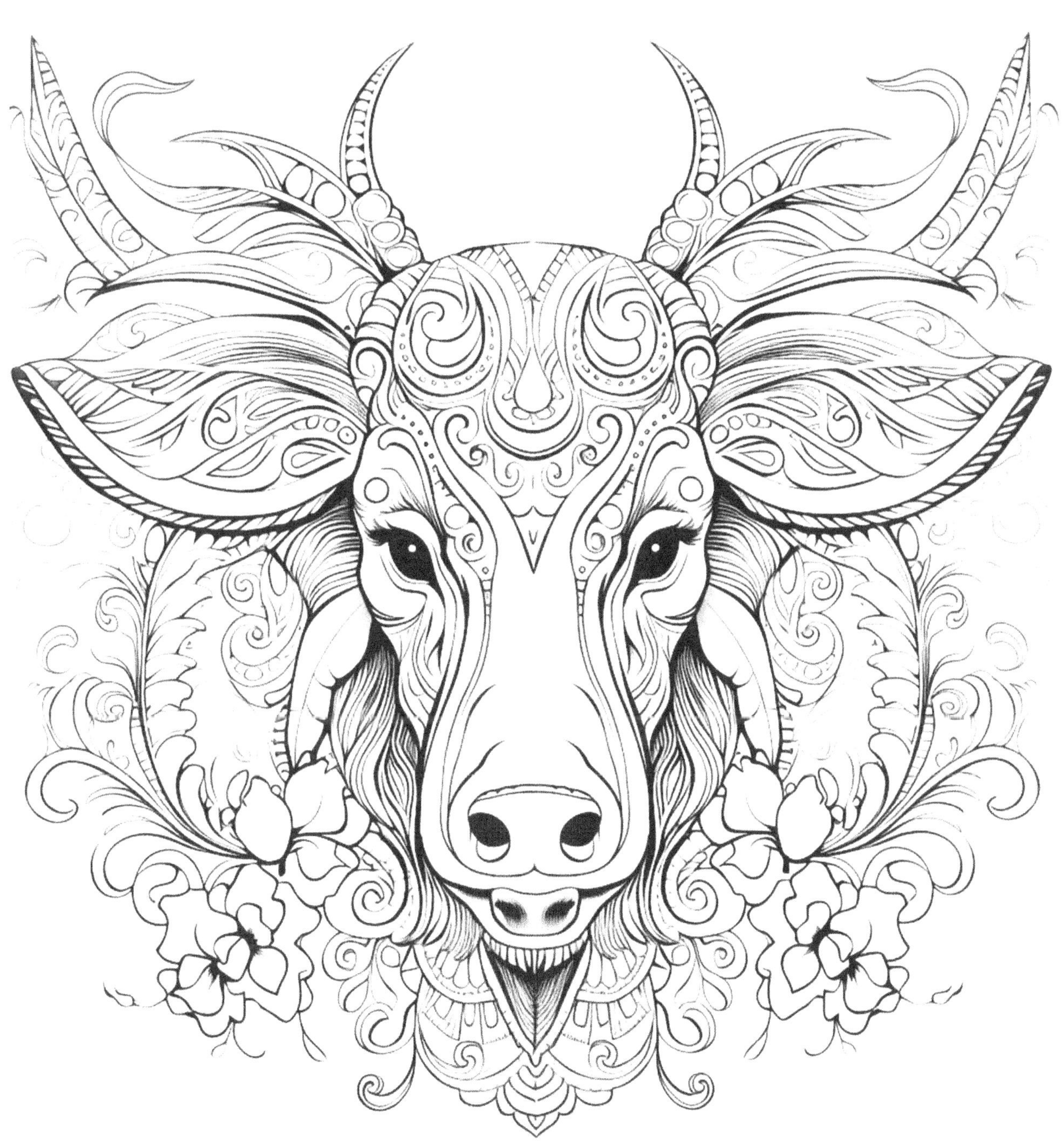

Color Test Pages

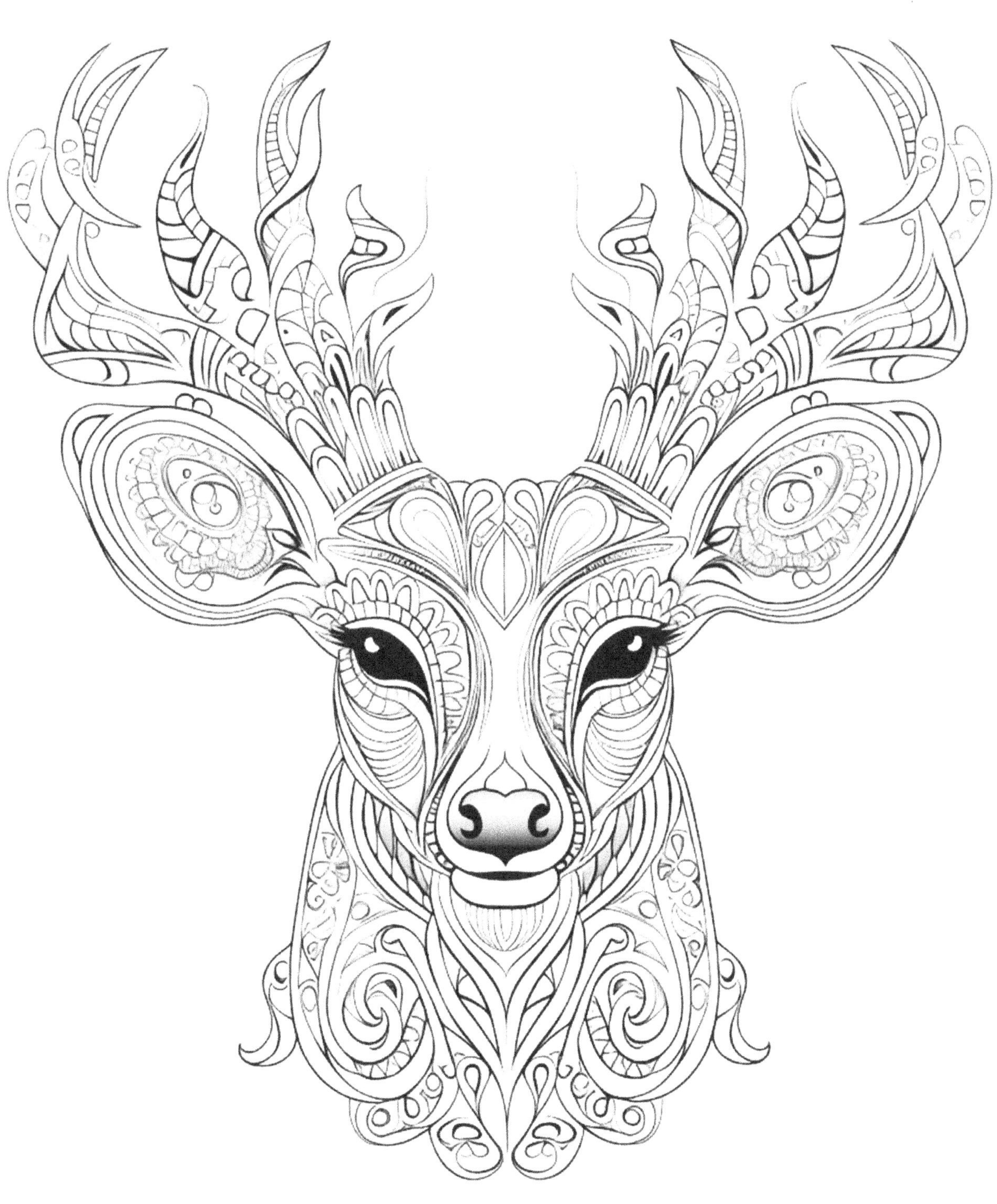

Color Test Pages

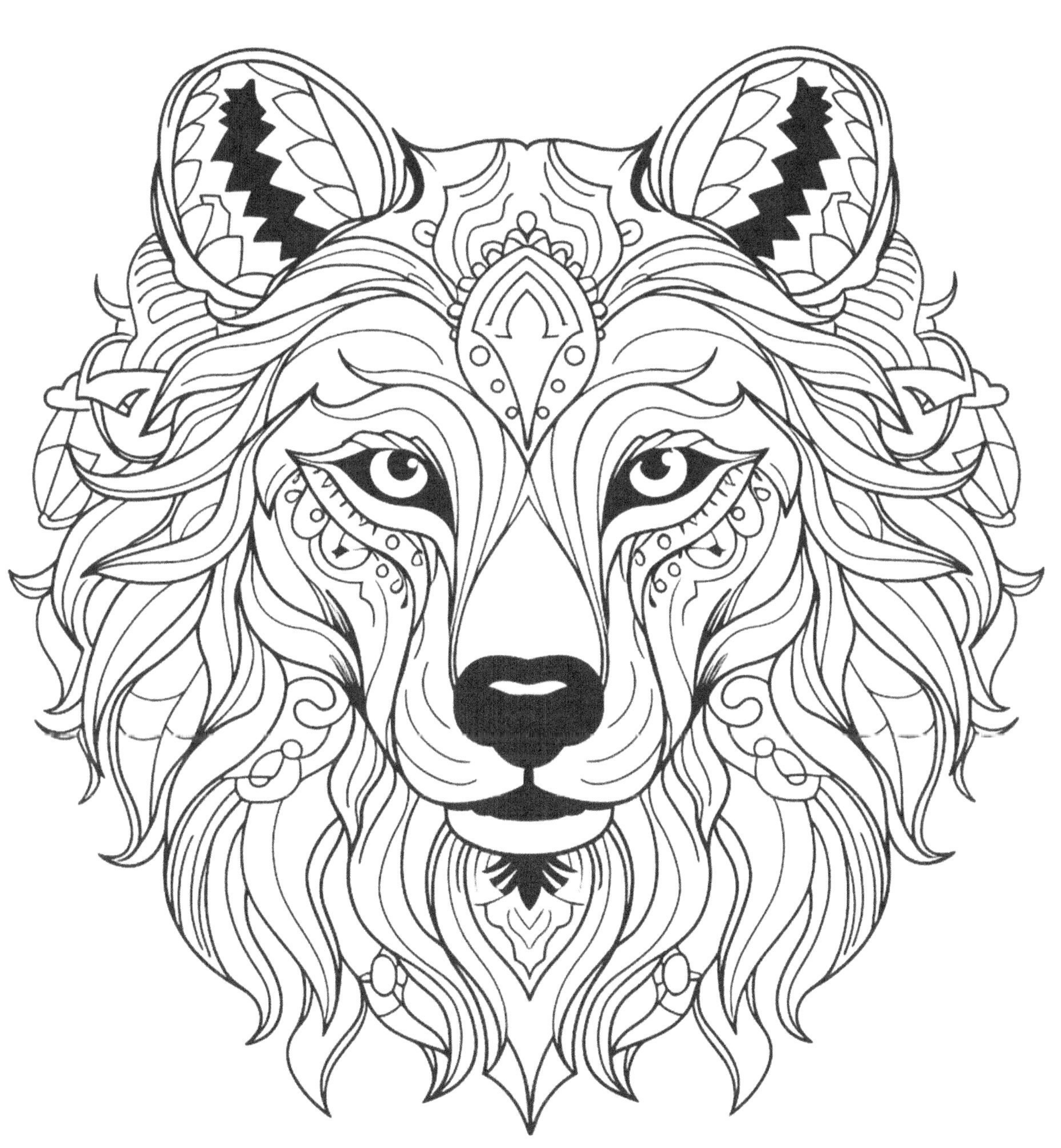

Color Test Pages

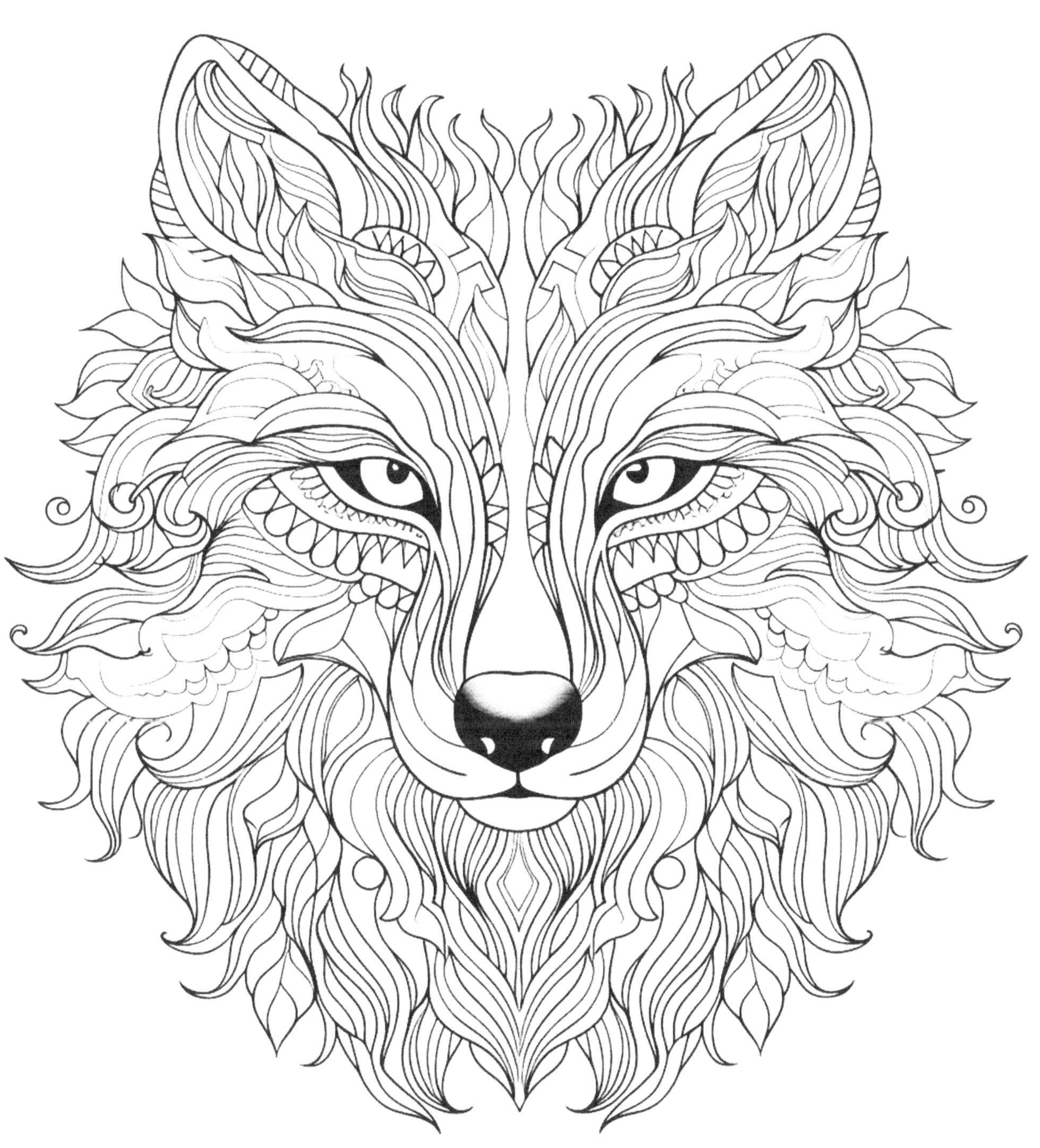

Color Test Pages

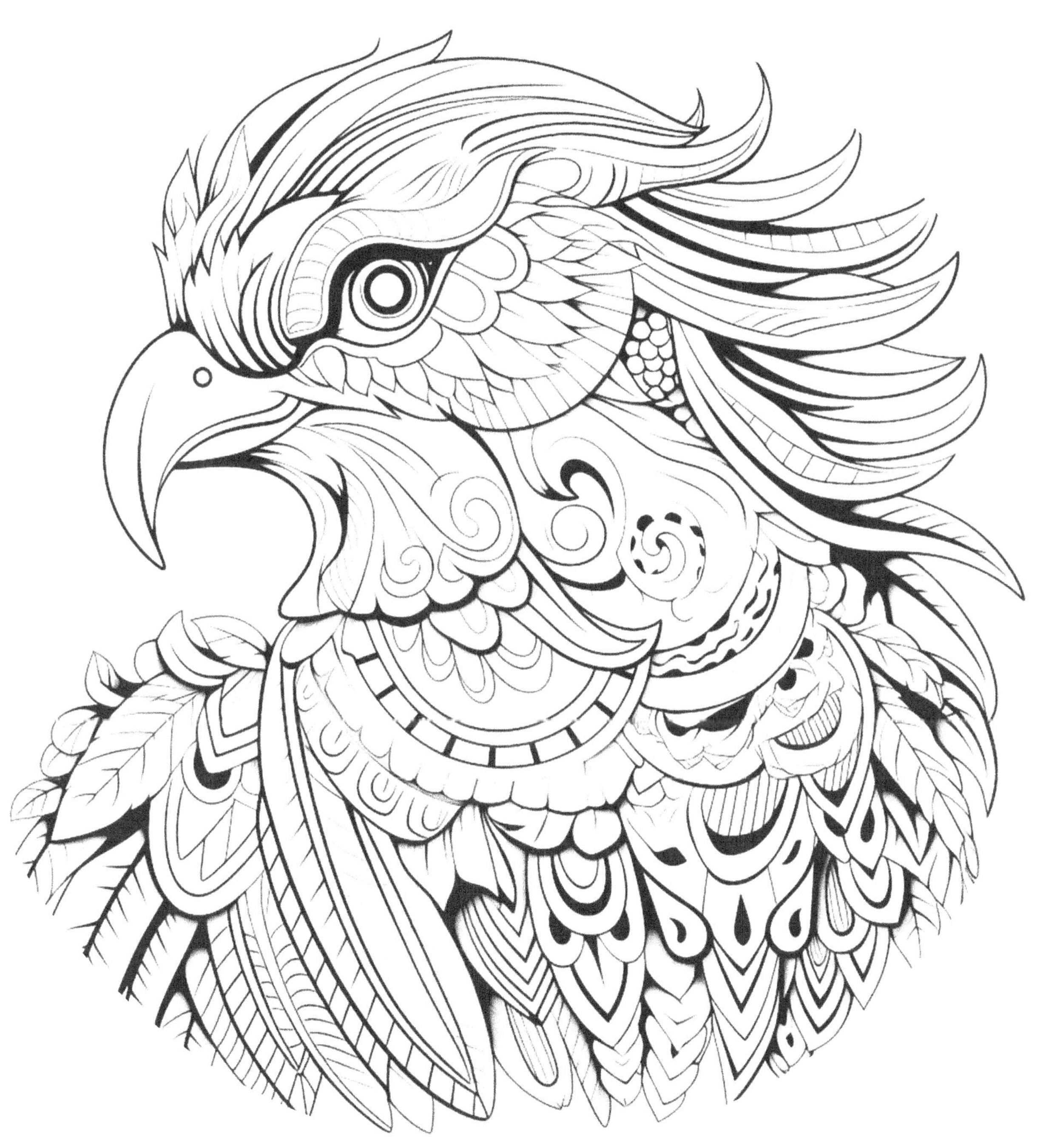

Color Test Pages

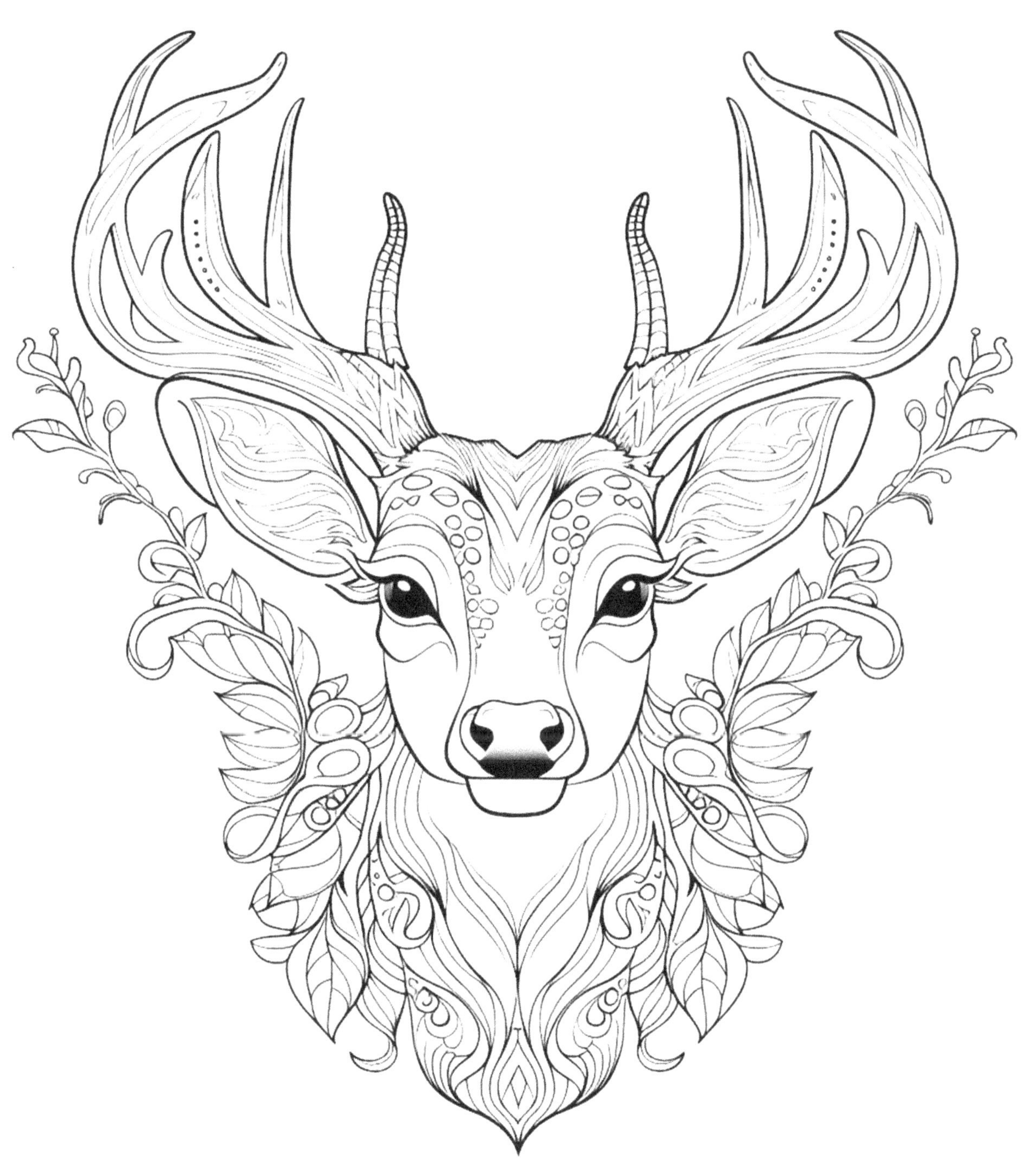

Color Test Pages

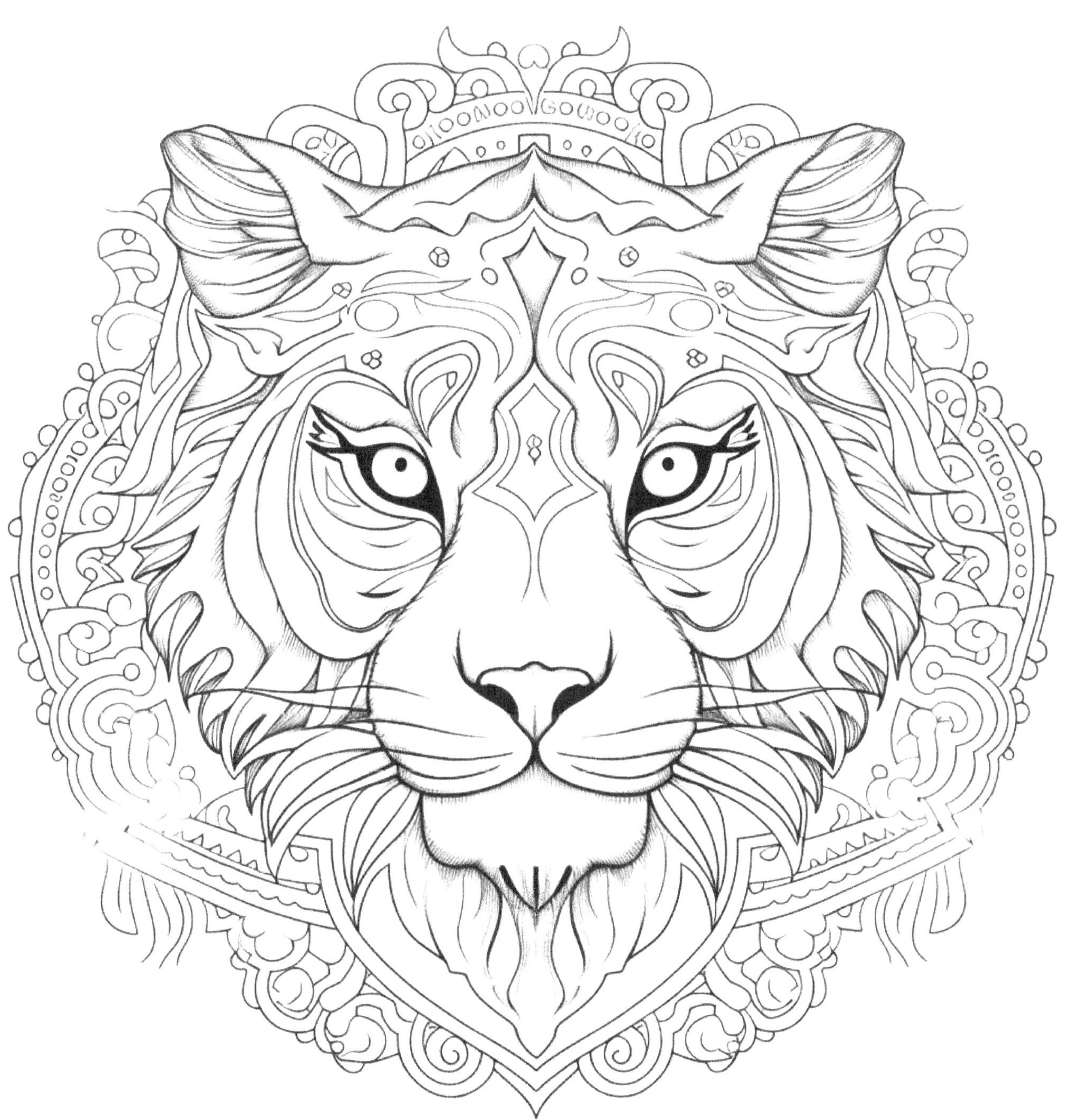

Color Test Pages

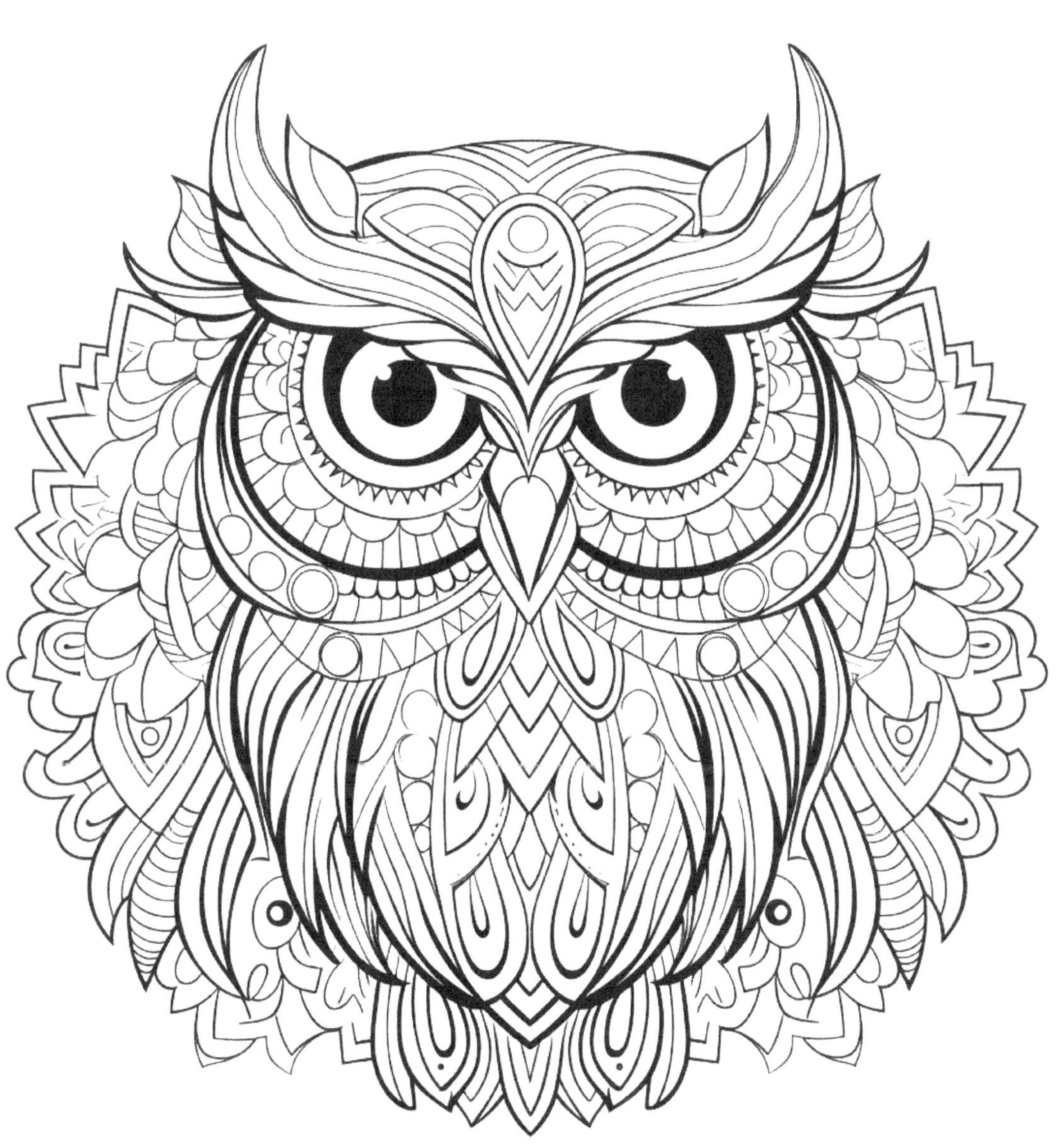

Color Test Pages

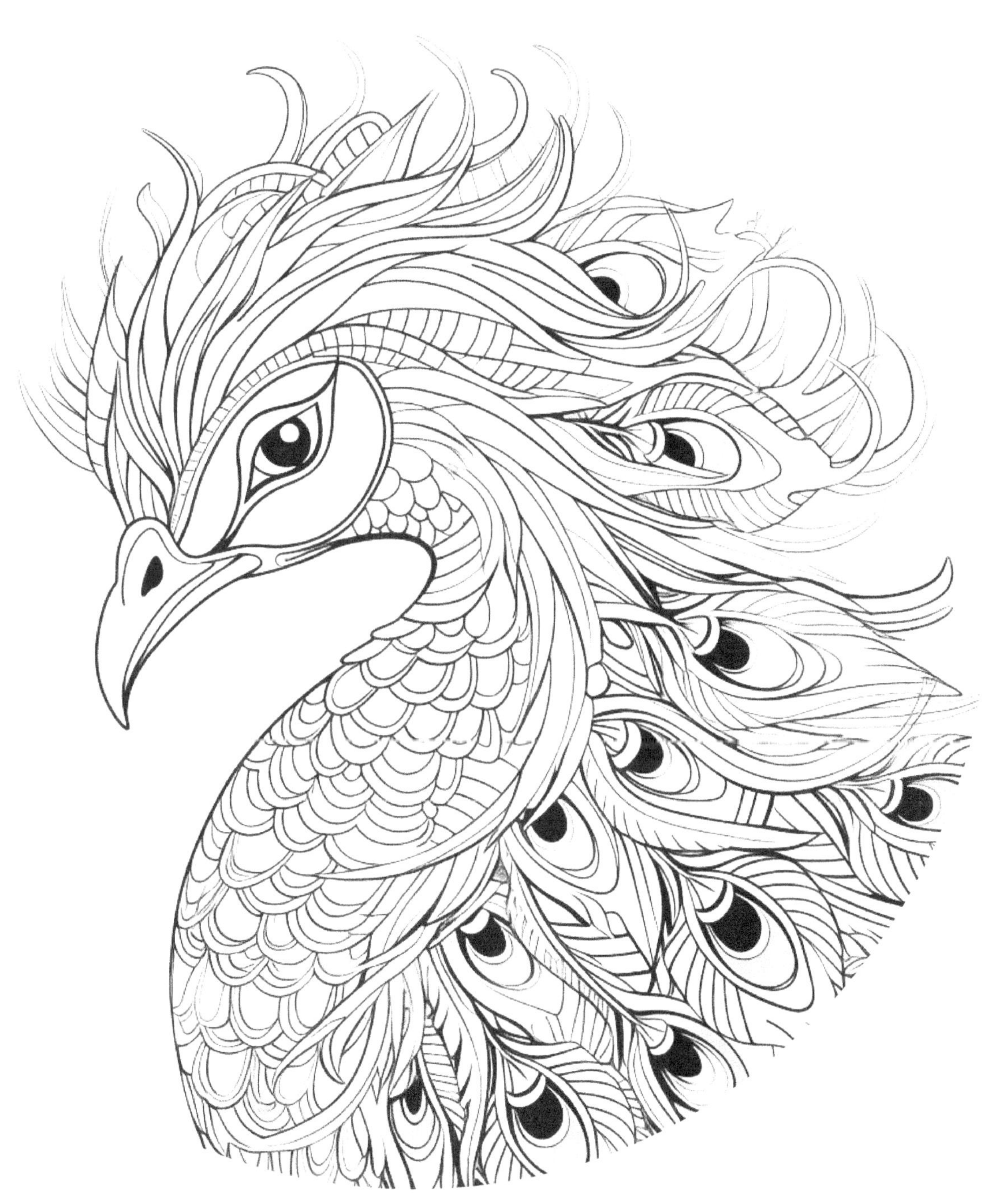

Color Test Pages

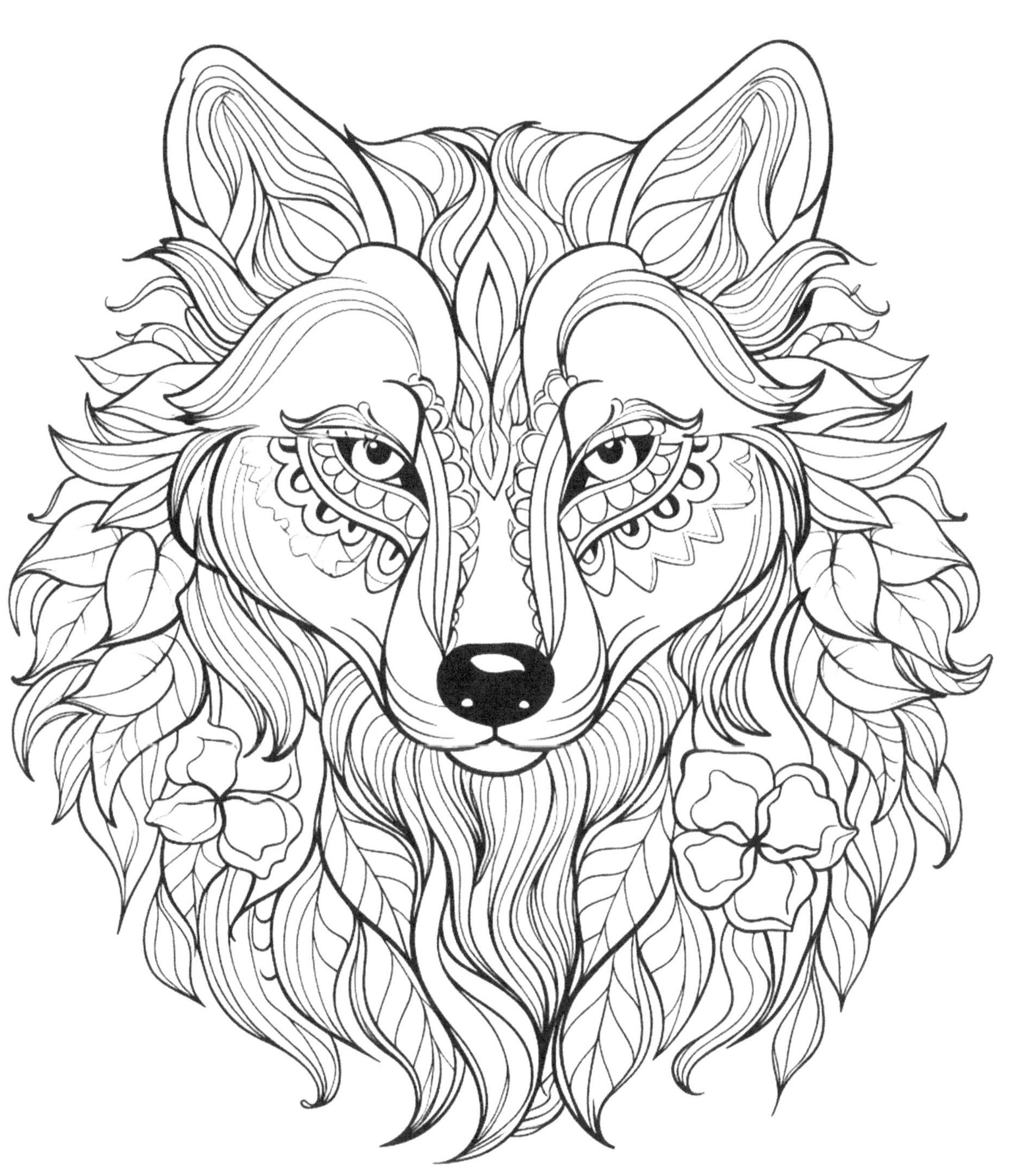

Color Test Pages

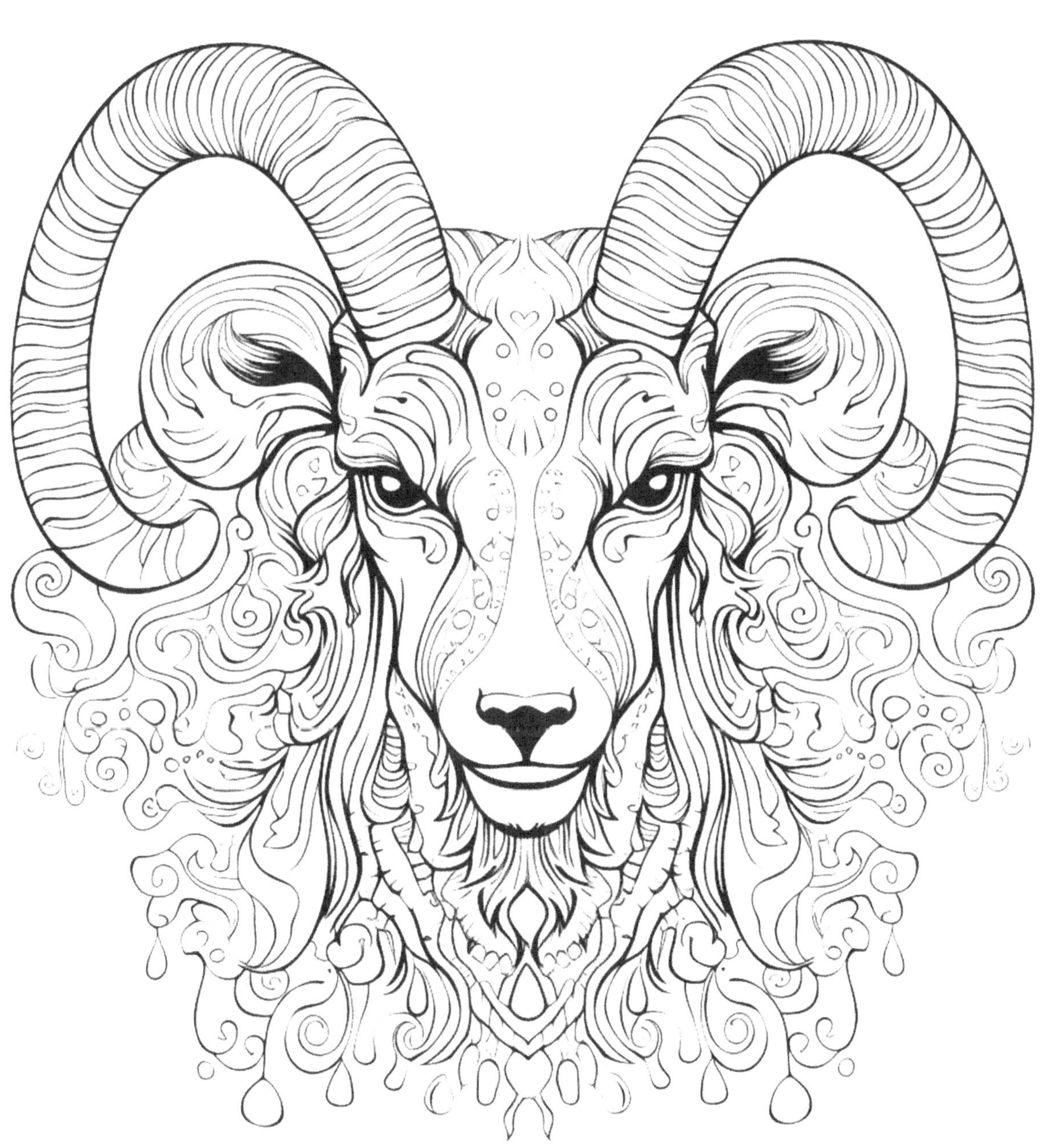

Color Test Pages

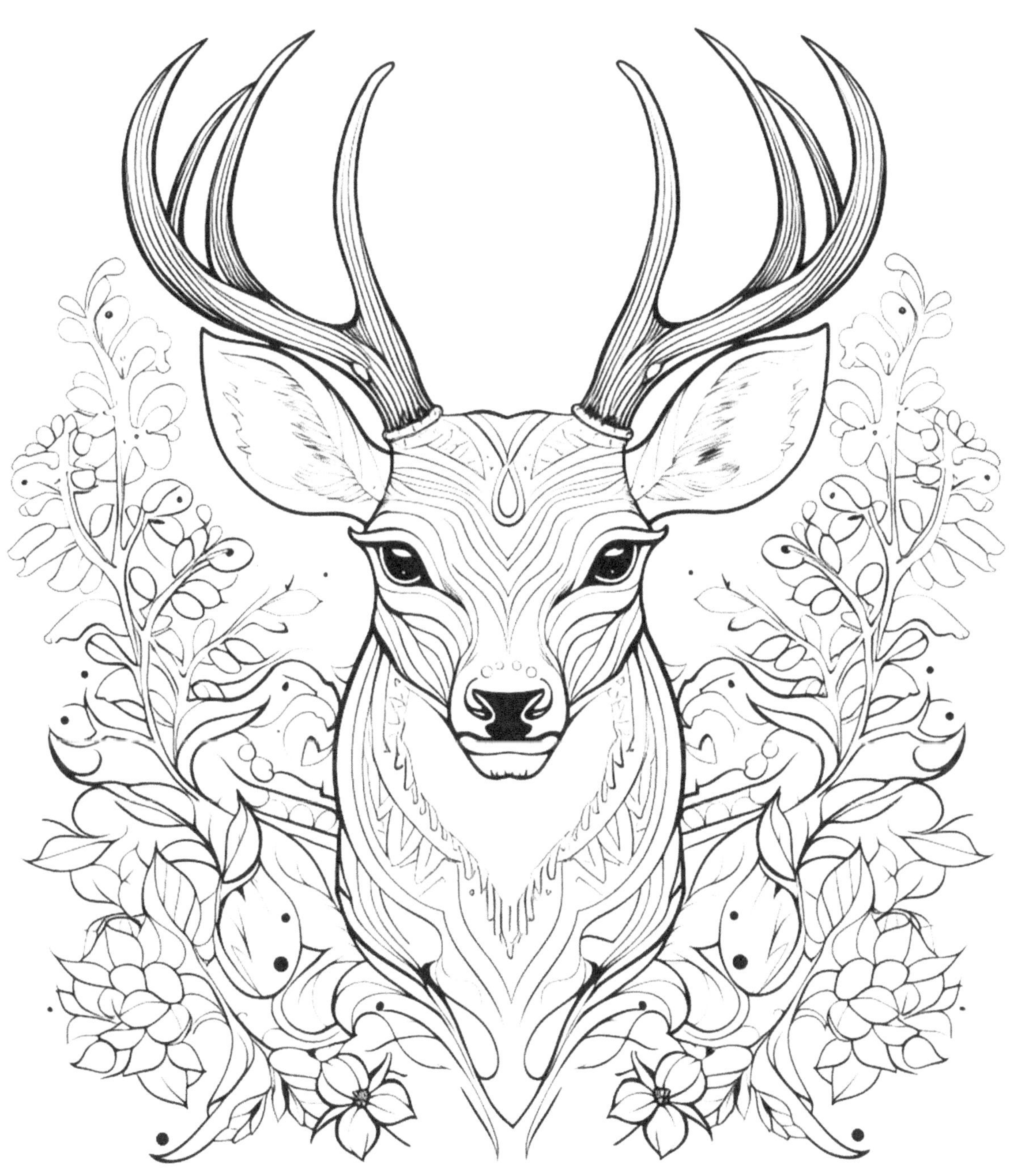

Color Test Pages

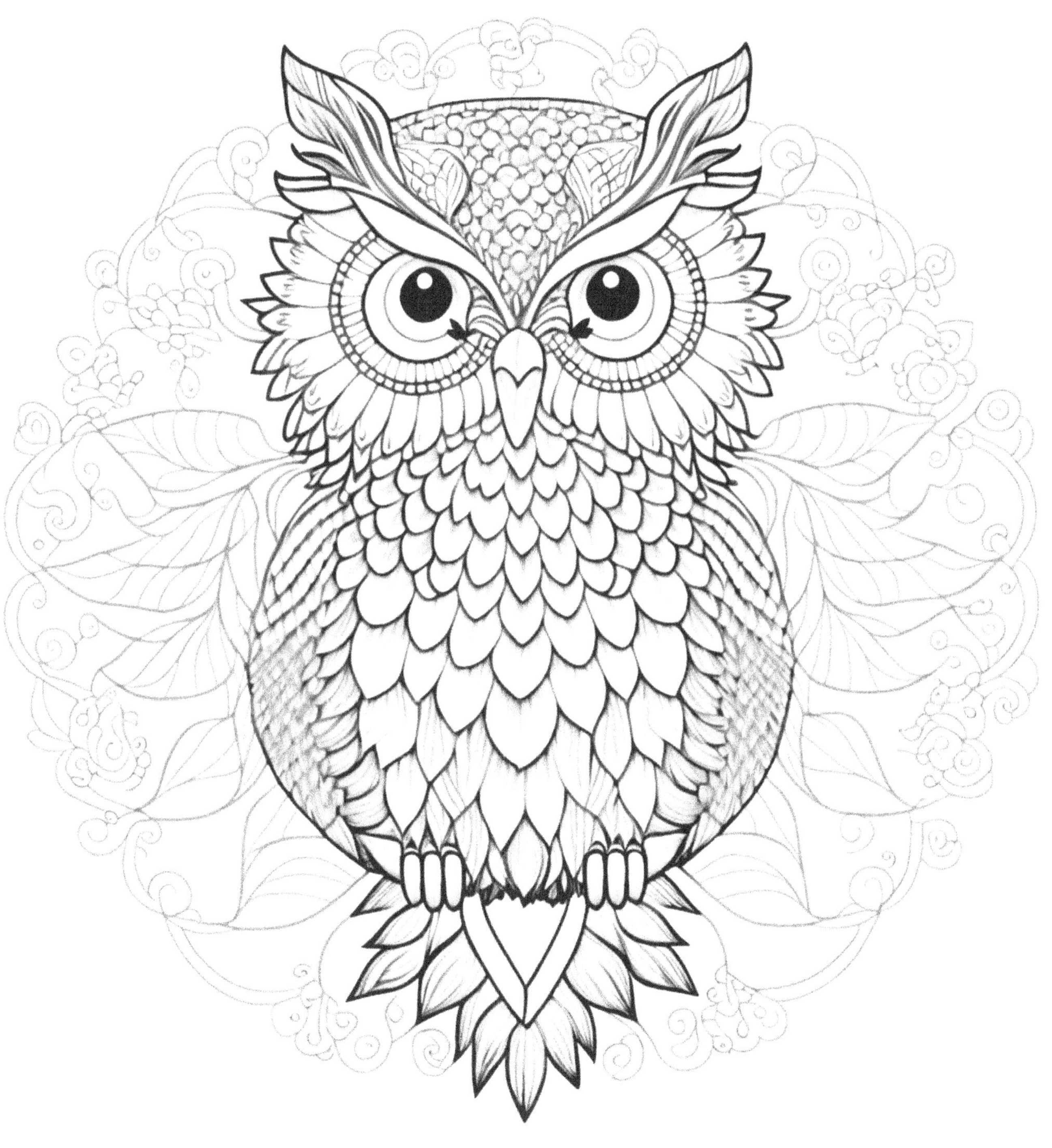

Color Test Pages

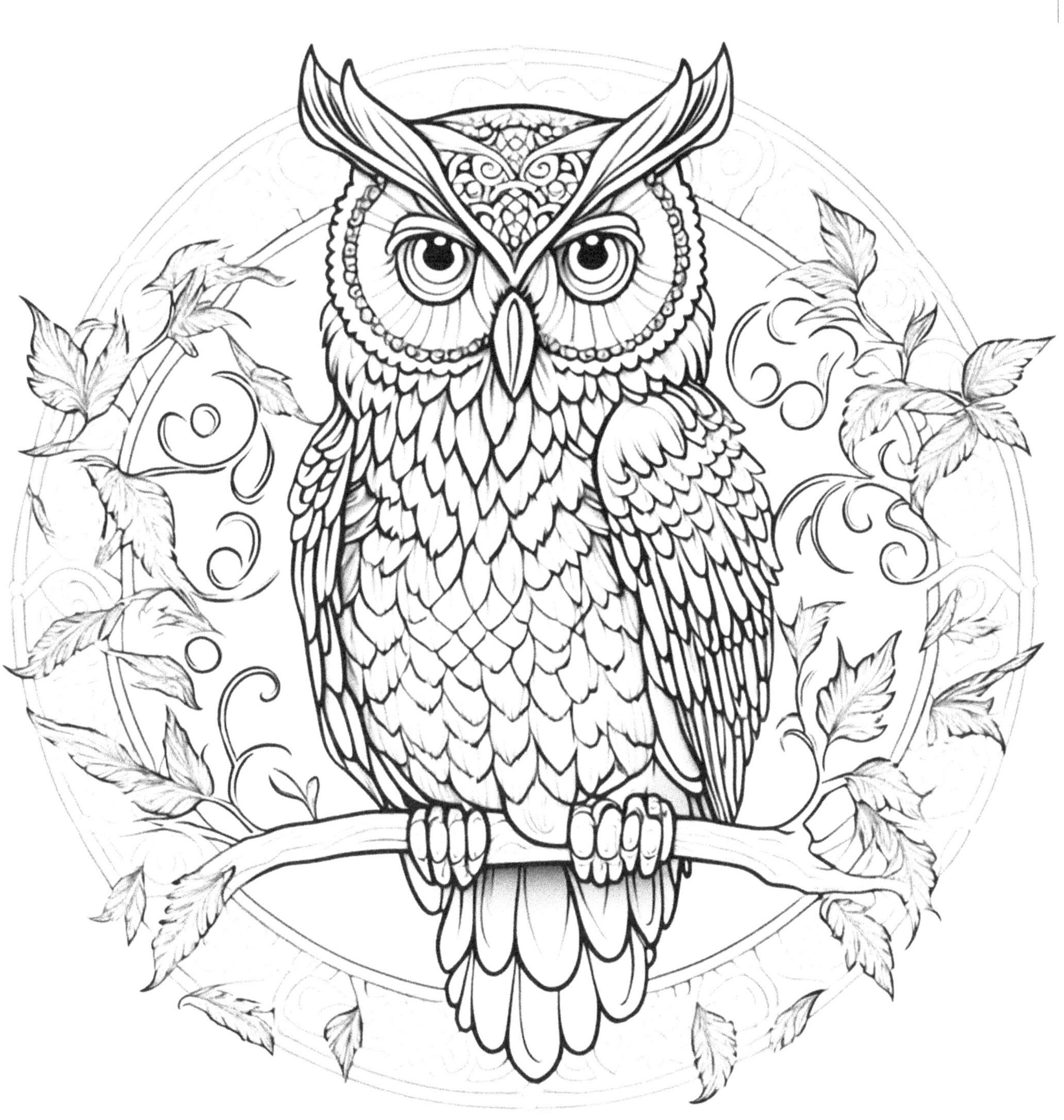

Color Test Pages

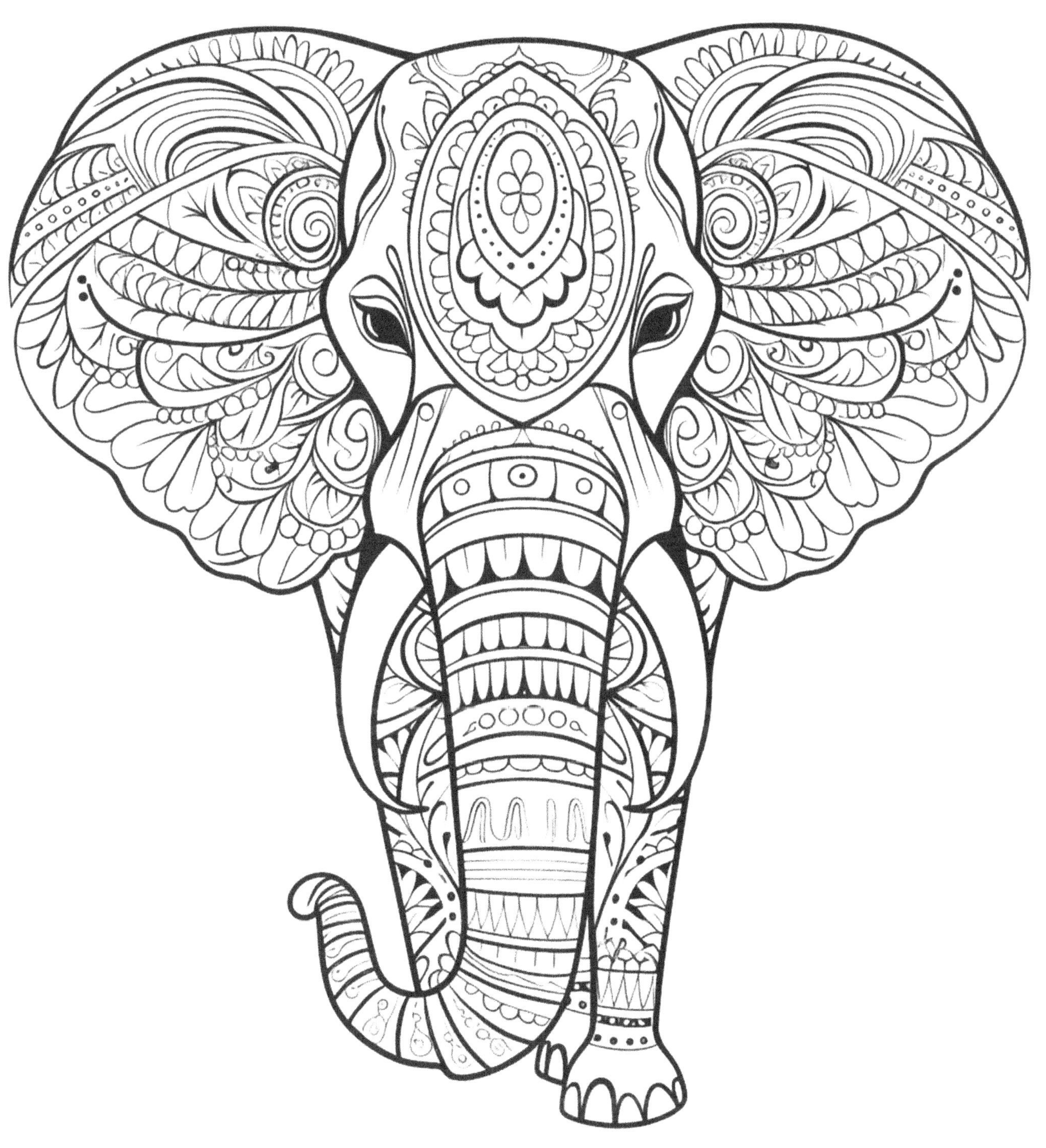

Color Test Pages

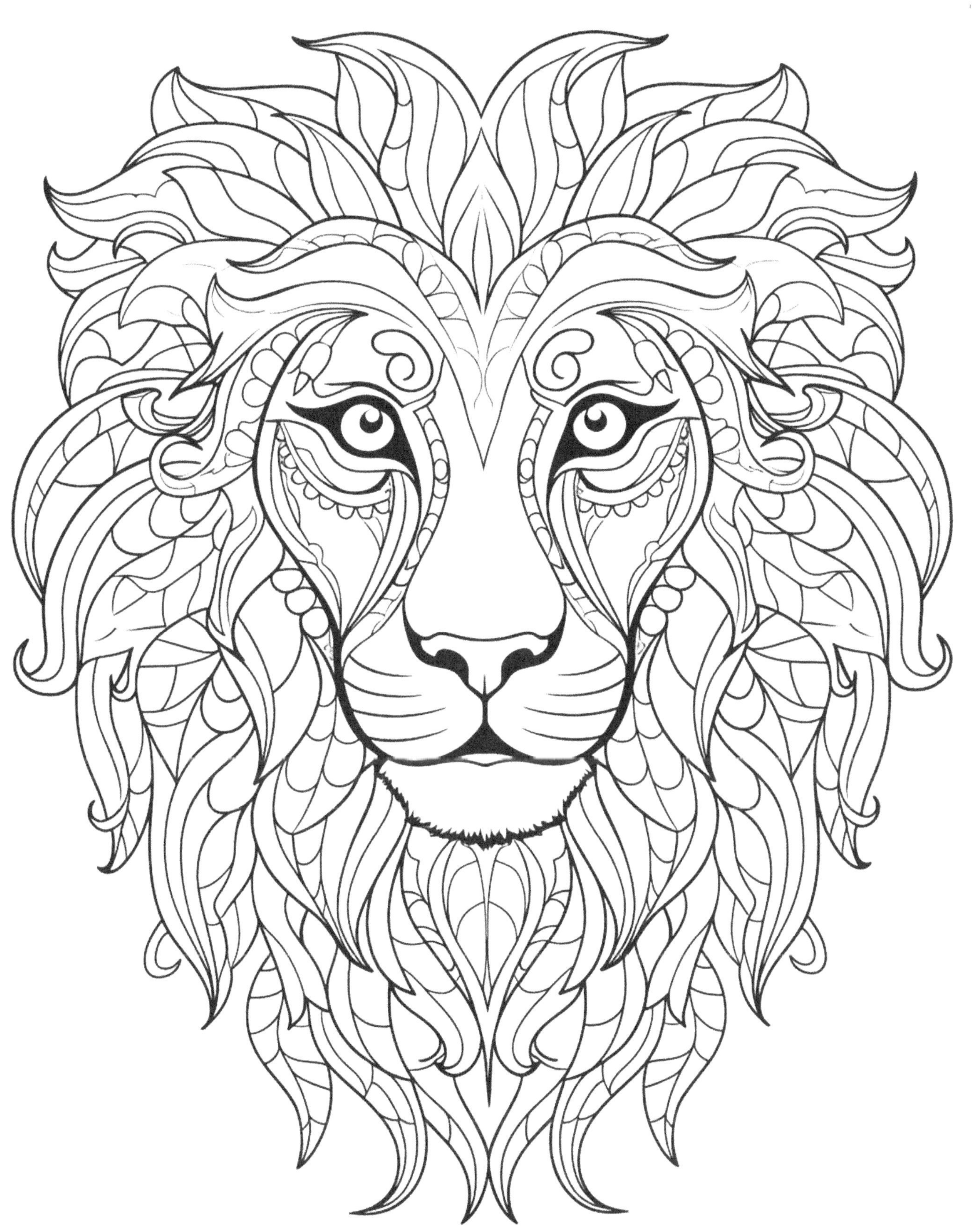

Color Test Pages

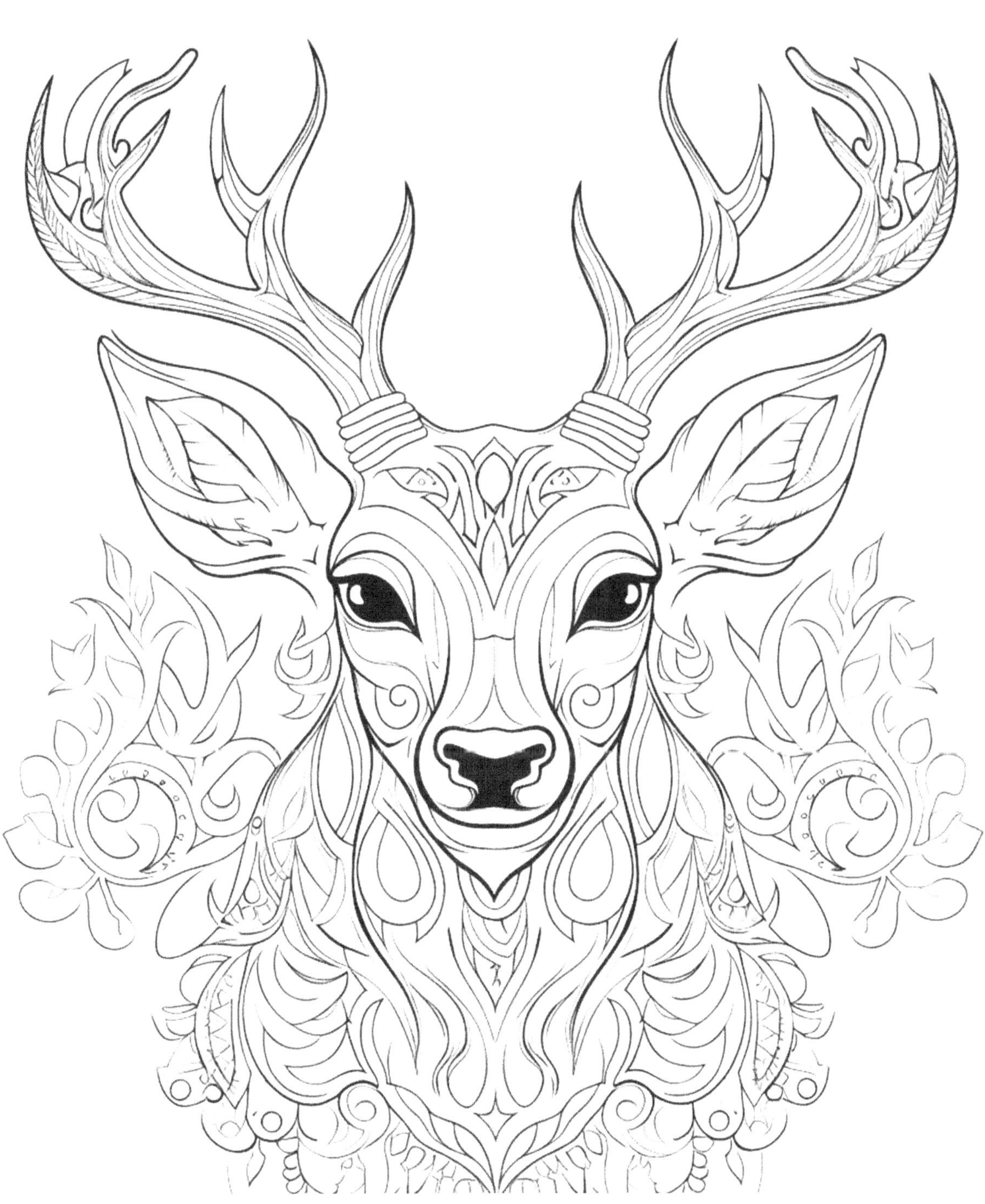

Color Test Pages

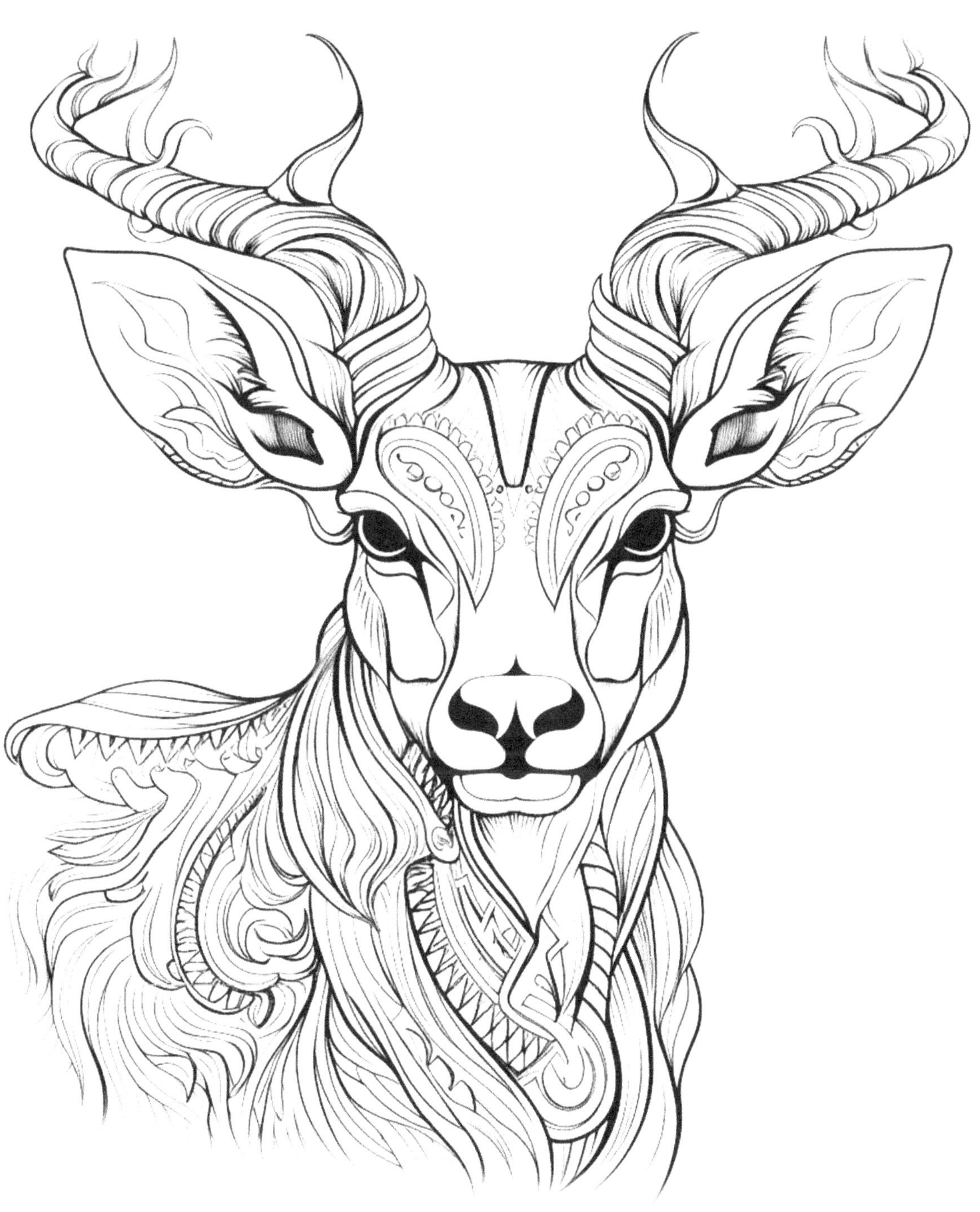

Color Test Pages

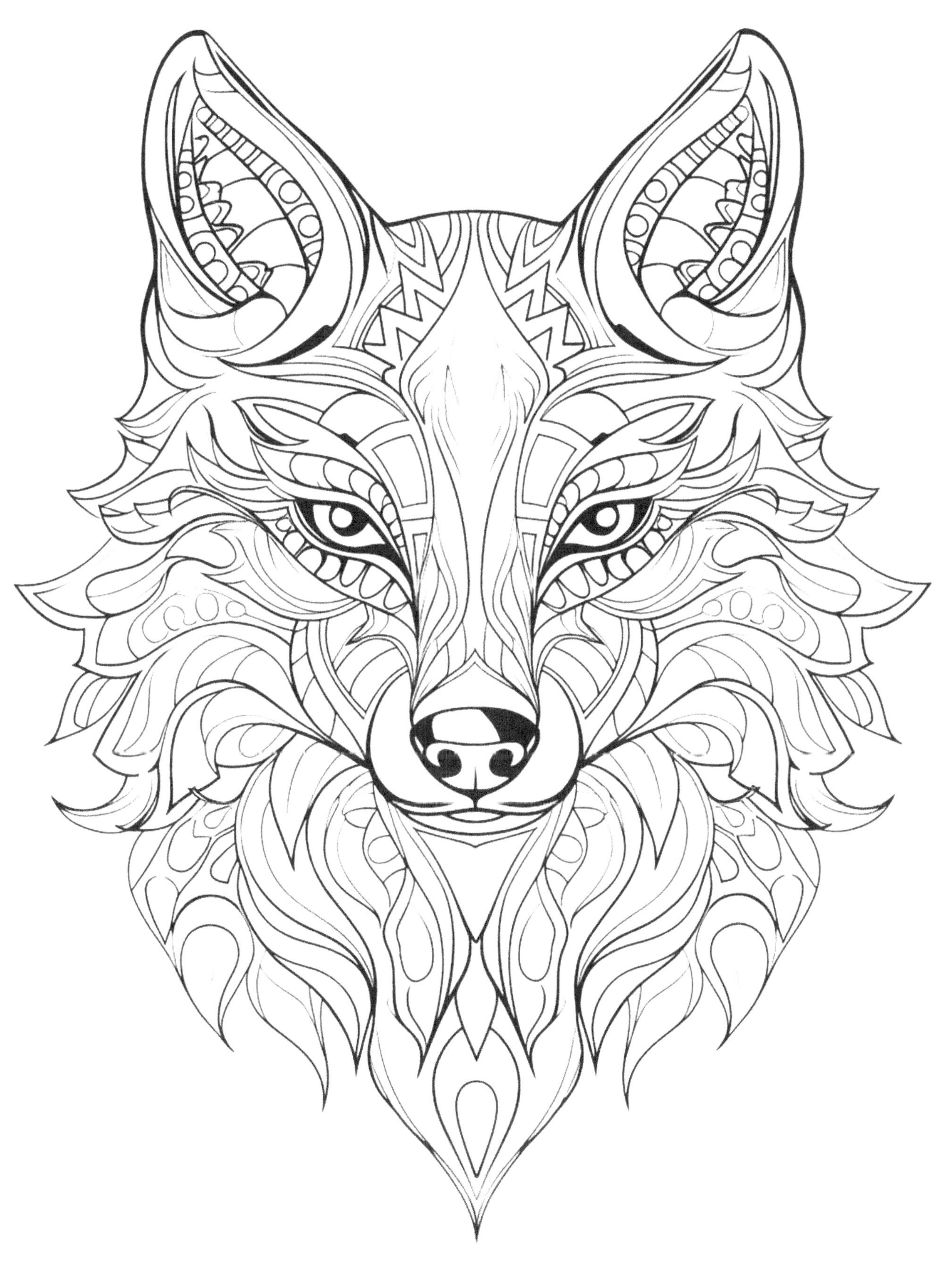

Color Test Pages

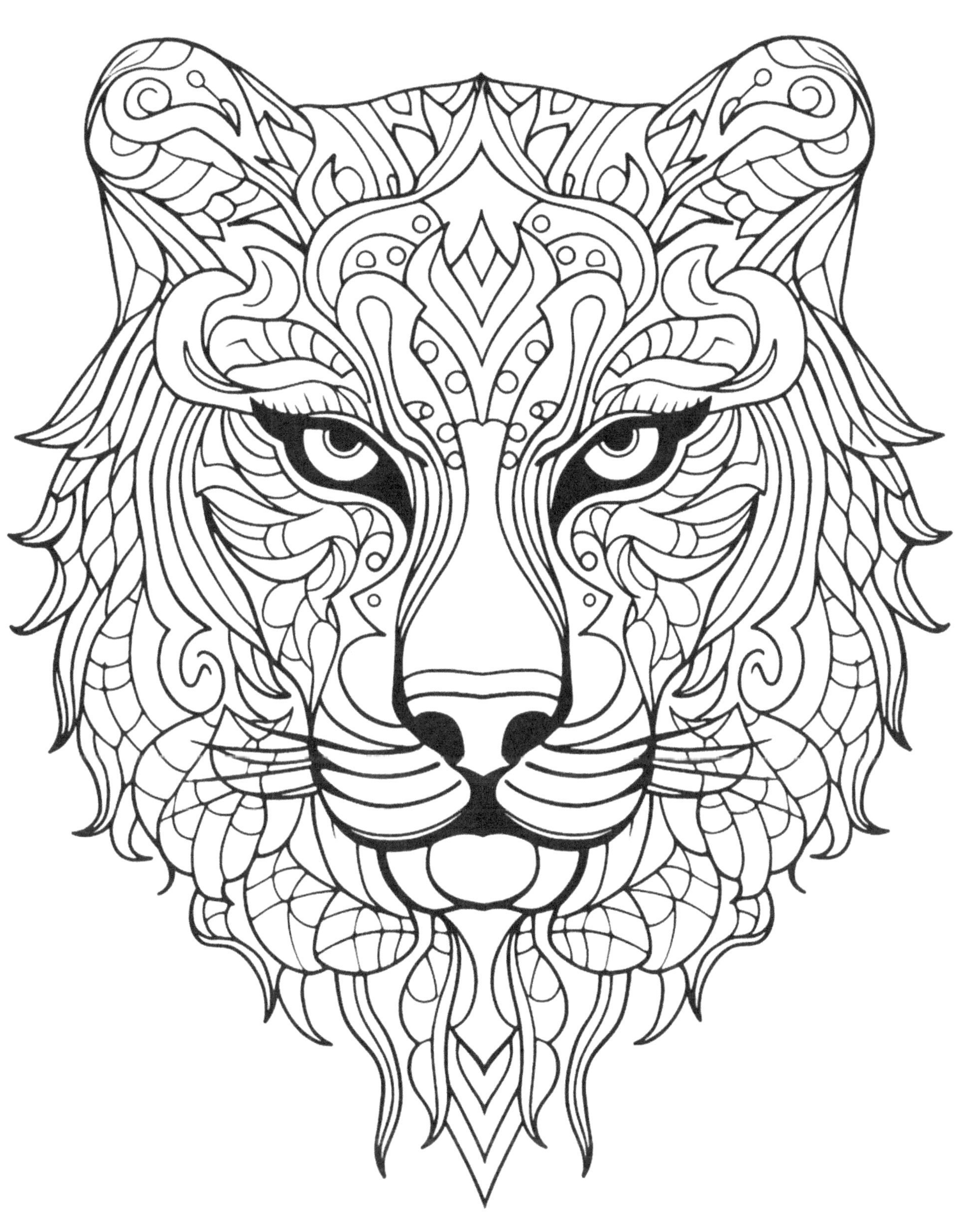

Color Test Pages

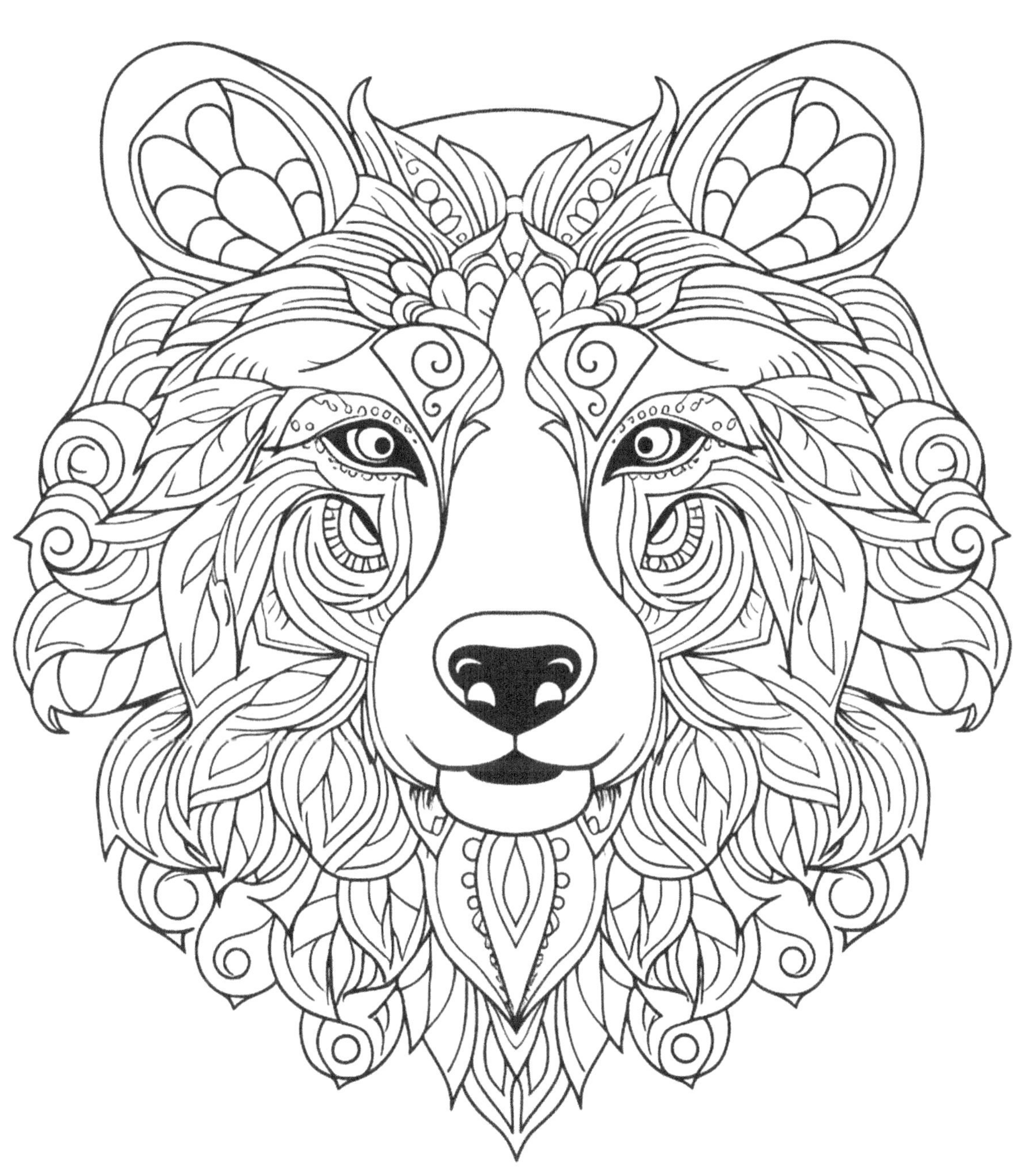

Color Test Pages

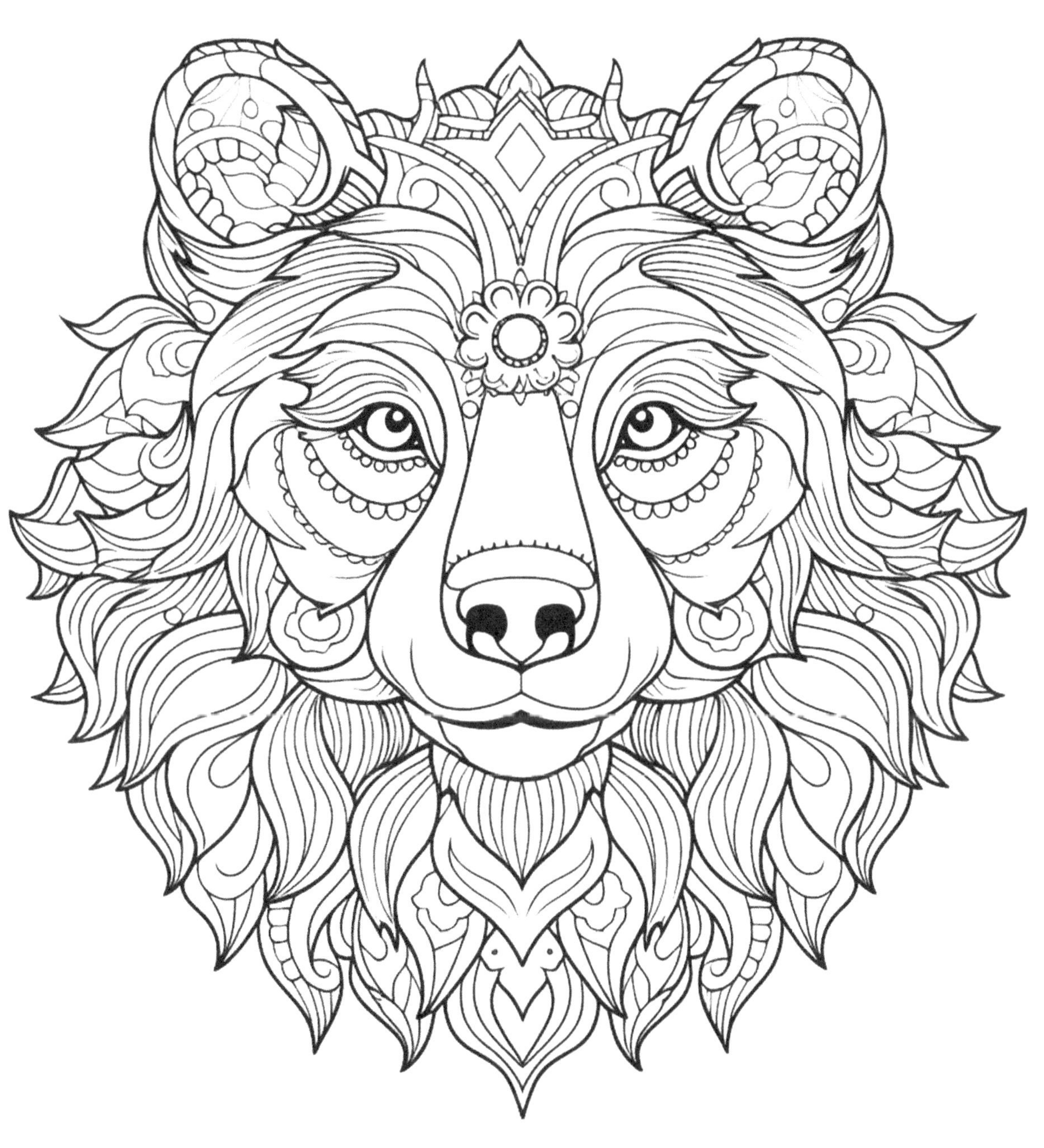

Color Test Pages

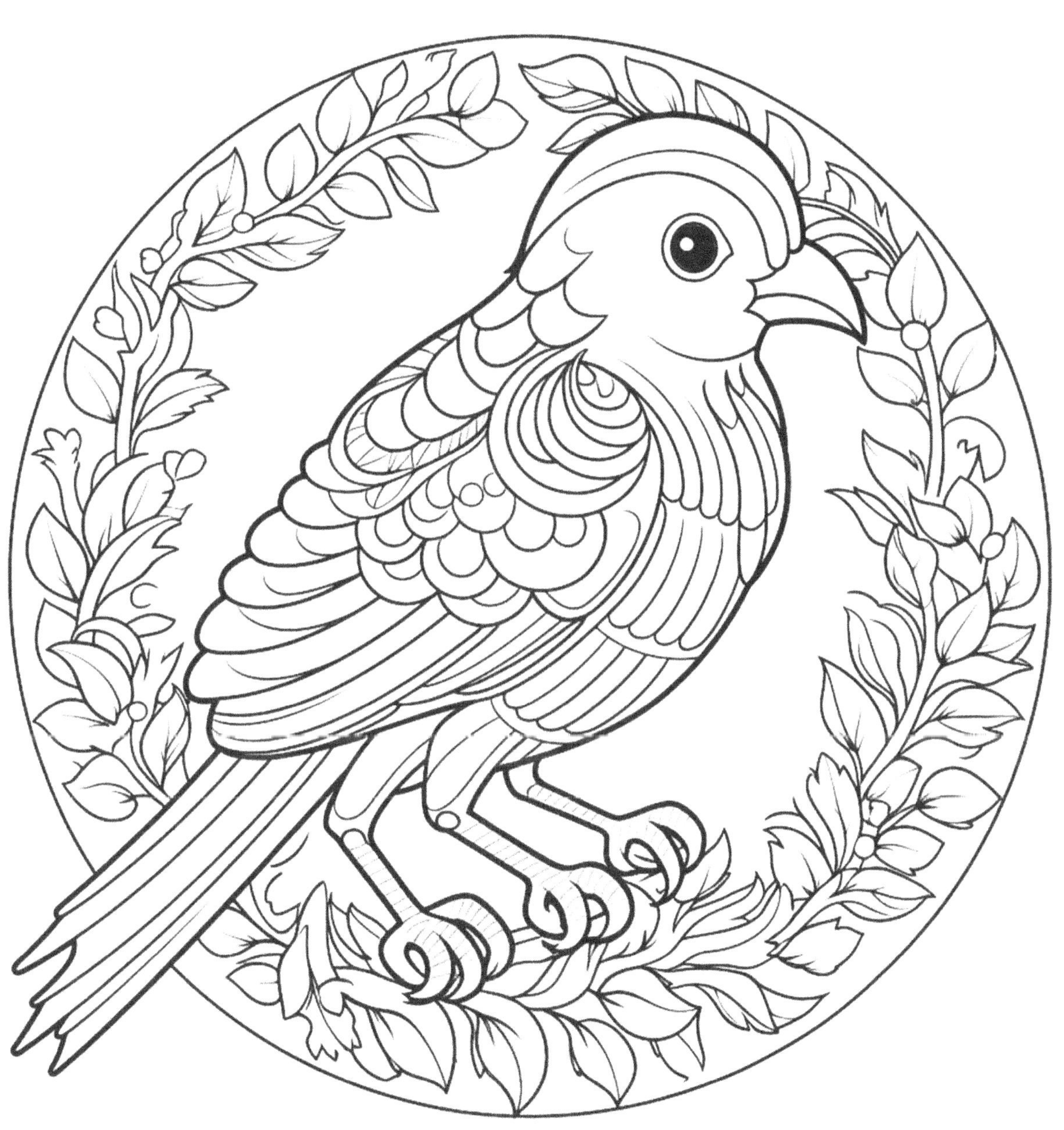

Color Test Pages

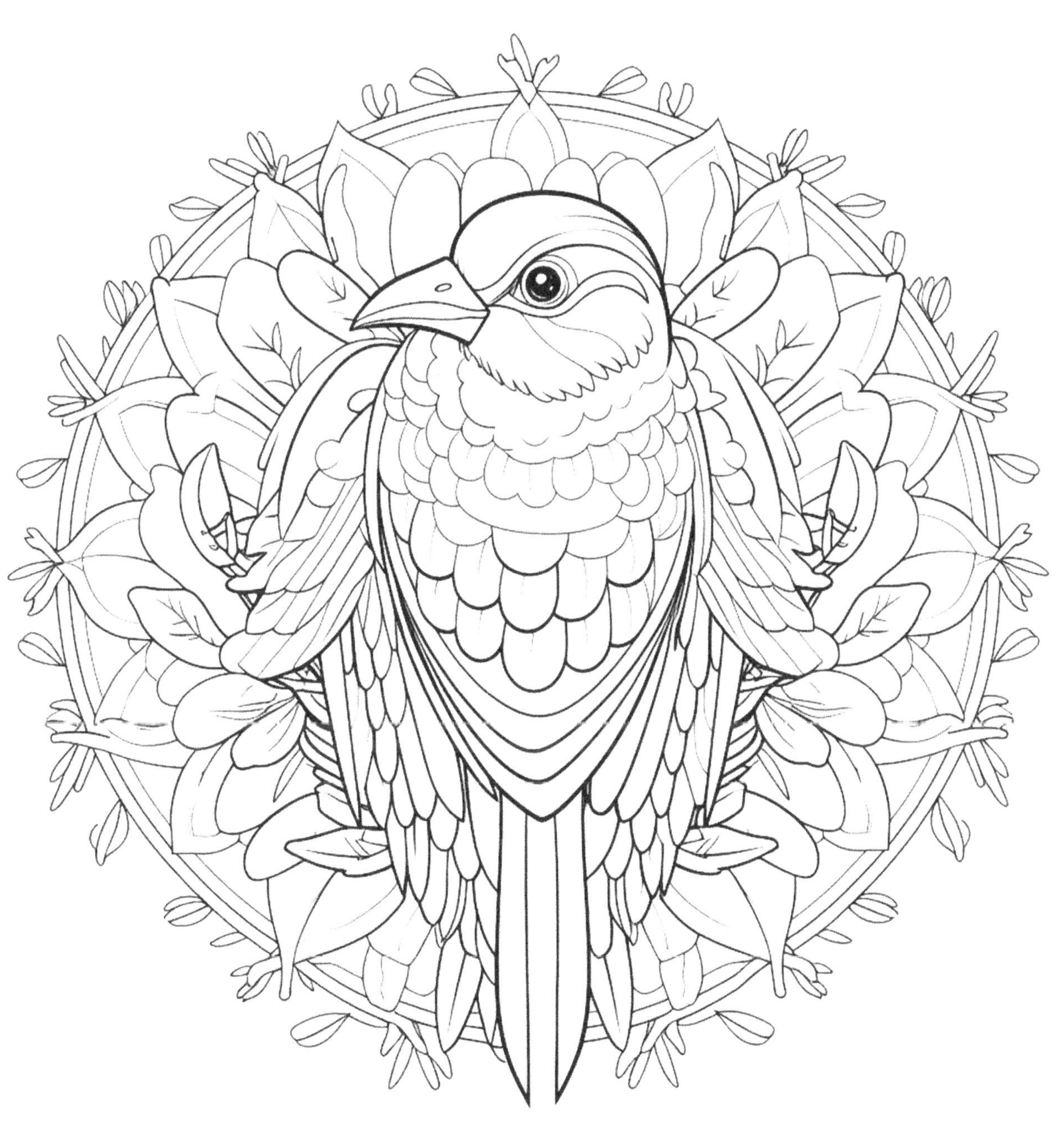

Color Test Pages

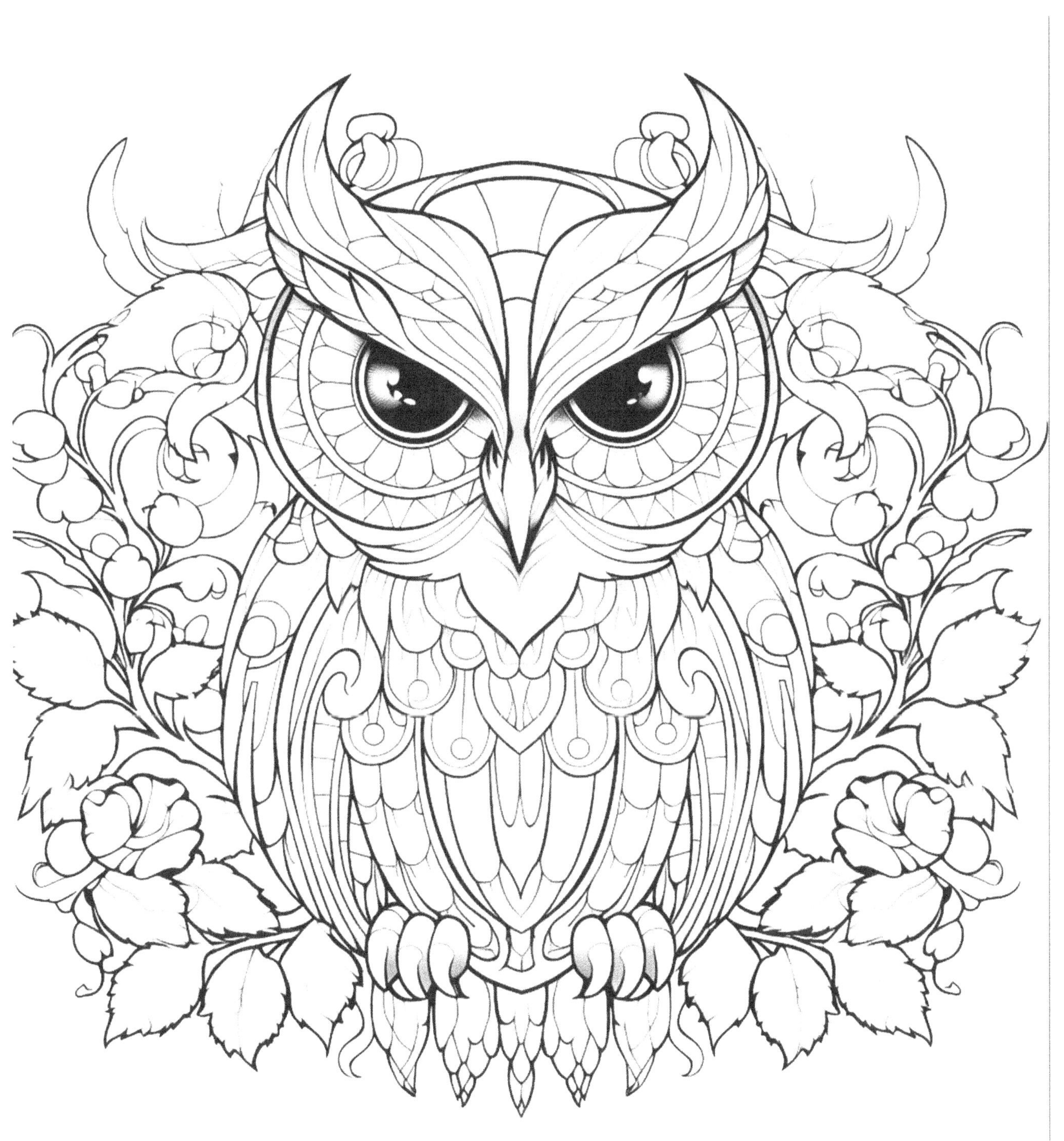

Color Test Pages

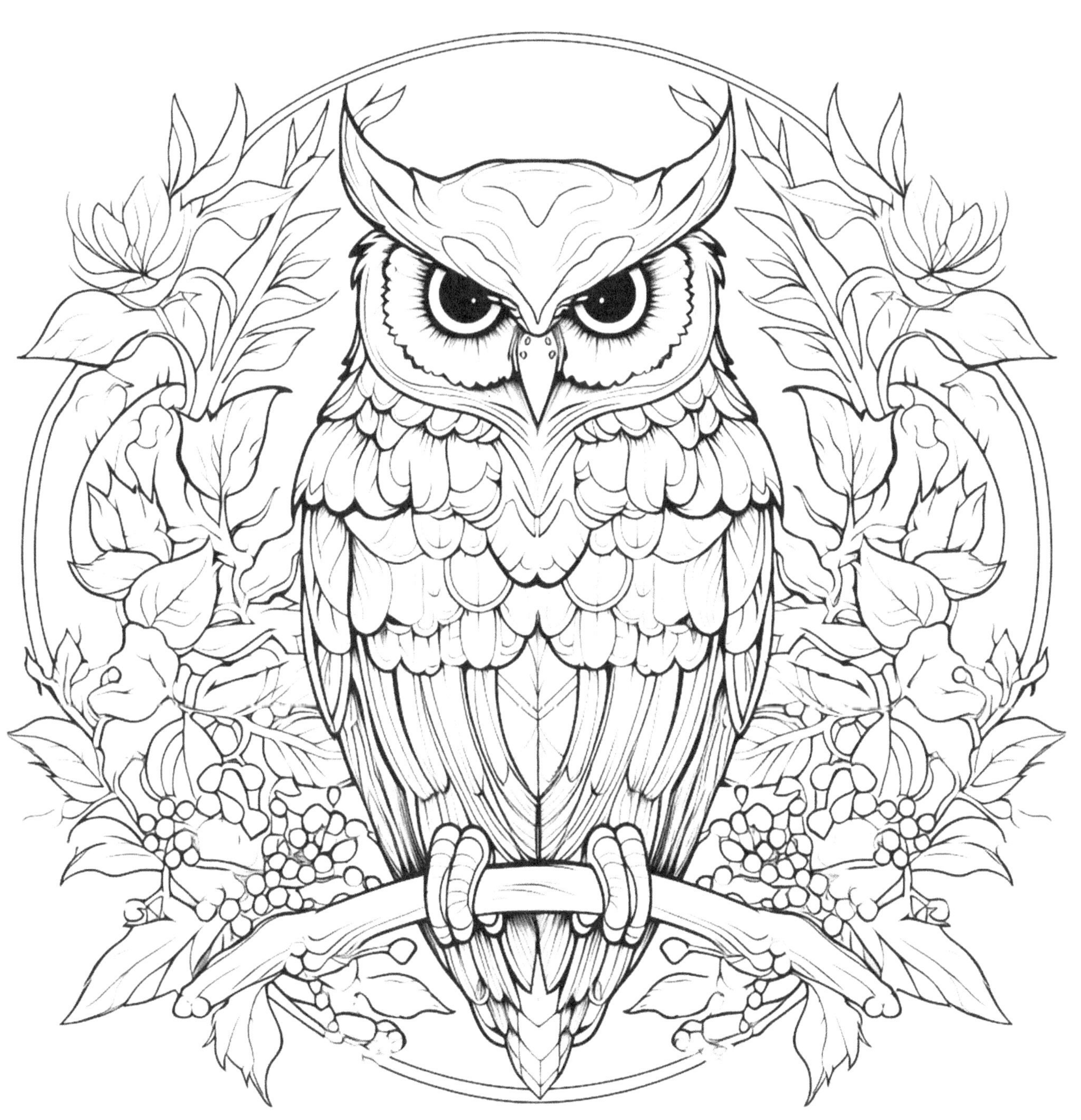

Color Test Pages

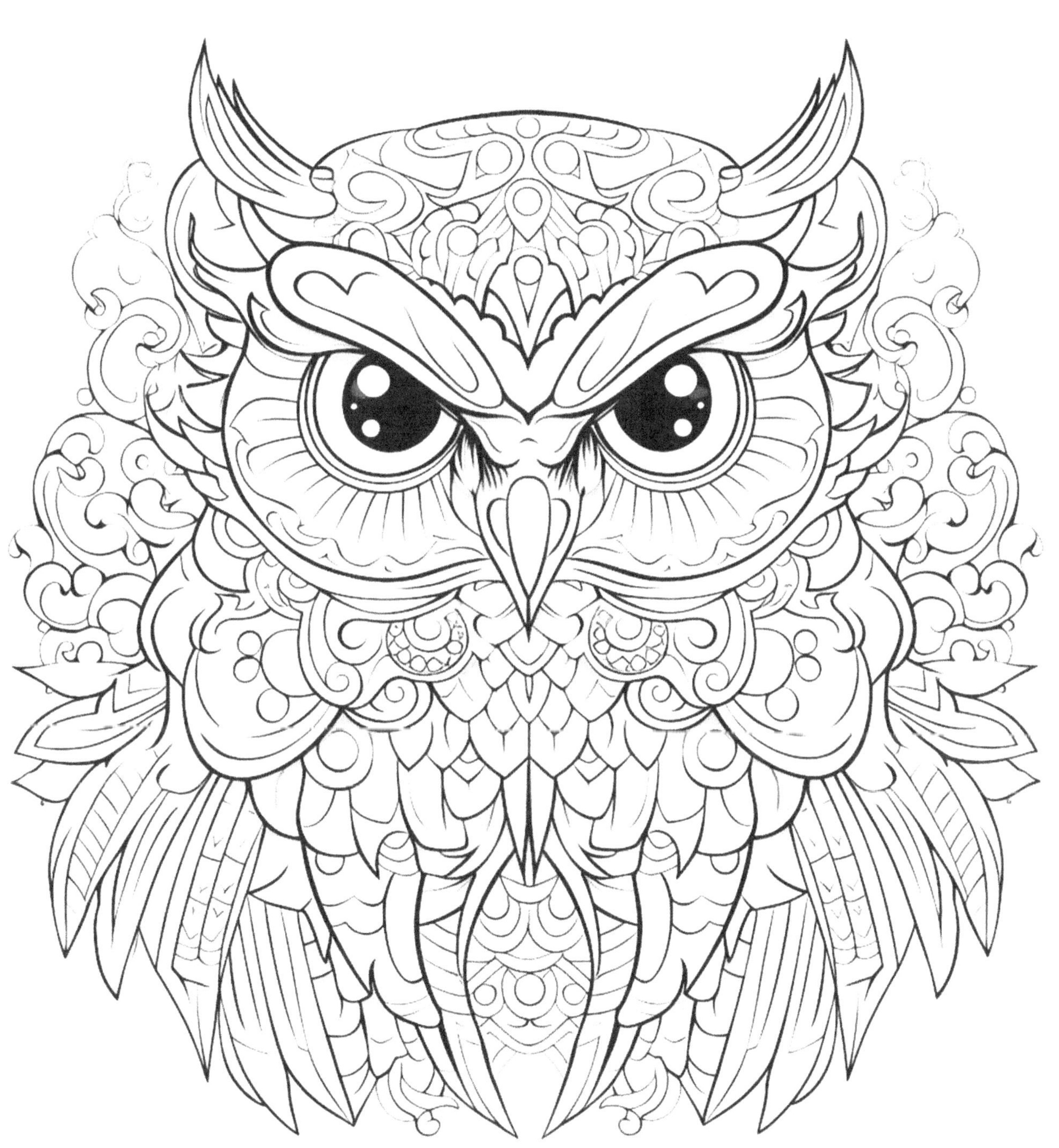

Color Test Pages

Hello!

As an independent author of my coloring book, I want to sincerely thank you for your support and purchase. I hope you enjoy my book as much as I enjoyed creating it.

As an independent author, I greatly value the opinions and comments of my readers. If you enjoyed my book, I would greatly appreciate it if you could leave an online review. Not only would it help me grow as an author, but it would also help other readers find my book and enjoy it as much as you did.

Thank you again for your support and for helping my anime coloring book reach more people.

Sincerely,

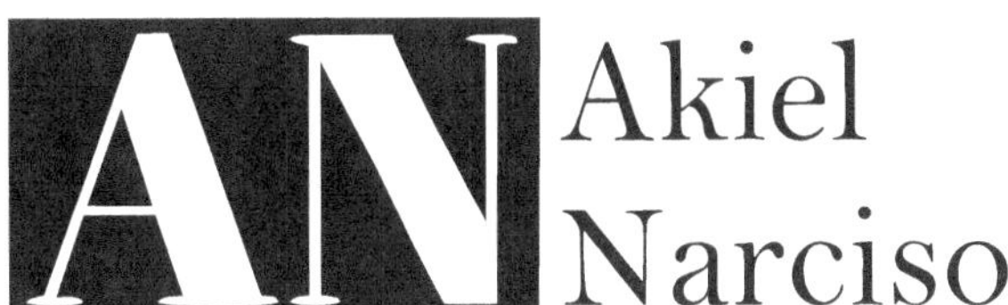